Graham Greene

A Study in His Language and Style

Graham Greene

A Study in His Language and Style

DURGA BHAVANI

PRESTIGE

PRESTIGE BOOKS
3/28, East Patel Nagar
New Delhi 110 008

Published by Prestige Books, 1999

ISBN 81-7551-066-8

Composed by Pivot Computers, Delhi 110 006
Printed by Dhawan Industries Offset, New Delhi 110 028

Contents

PART II

The Presentation of Speech in Greene's Novels 50

To
the memory
of
my mother

Acknowledgements

I wish to thank all my friends and well-wishers who have rendered great help in writing this book; especially Professor N. Krishna Swamy for his valuable comments and Professor C. Vijayasri for her encouragement and guidance. I specially thank Prestige Books for bringing out the book so expeditiously.

Durga Bhavani

Foreword

What makes a verbal message a work of art, a thing of beauty, a text with a literary texture? It is truism to say that it is the special use of language that contributes to the literariness of a discourse or text; there is a strong connection between literariness, language and narrative modes but it is impossible to maintain a clear-cut distinction between ordinary communication and literary communication, between expository discourse and narrative discourse. Narration is like motion pictures; it keeps moving in space and time and between ideology and psychology. Narrative modes are "like oil in cooking. You cannot have it on its own"—to borrow a metaphor from Roman Jacobson. The language of literature is more delphic (i.e. obscure, ambiguous, oracular, suggestive) and its study raises more questions than it answers.

Durga Bhavani's study of Graham Greene's narrative methods represents fine blending of stylistics and literary interpretation. Her book *Graham Greene: A Study in His Language and Style* makes use of developments in 'New Stylistics' discourse analysis, Speech Act Theory, to name some important developments, and studies the presentation of speech and thought in Graham Greene's novels with reference to the stylistic strategies and narrative techniques employed by Greene; in addition, Durga Bhavani also brings out the pedagogic implications of such studies.

I am sure the book will be of use to all those who are interested in the study of literature and the teaching of literature and pave the way for many such studies.

I strongly recommend this book to all teachers, students

and researchers in the field of stylistics, literary studies and language teaching.

N. Krishna Swamy
Former Professor
CIEFL, Hyderabad

Introduction

This book has been inspired by 'New Stylistics' which has applied techniques and concepts of modern linguistics to the study of literature. The focus is on the social role of language rather than the formal and cognitive aspects of it. Halliday's (1973) functional model which sees languages as a 'social semiotic' is another source of inspiration for this book where the concentration is on the communicative and socially expressive functions of language. Halliday's contention is that language is multifunctional which means that even the simplest utterance 'Is your father feeling better' may be referential (referring to his father's illness), directive (demanding a reply from the hearer) and social (maintaining a sympathy bond between speaker and hearer). Thus, some kinds of language have a referential function (e.g. newspaper reports), others have a directive or persuasive function (e.g. advertising) and some others have an emotive or social function (e.g. casual conversation).

The functional classification of language is extended to literary studies as well. Halliday recognised that different kinds of literary writing may foreground different functions. His functional model of language acknowledges three major functions which he calls ideational, interpersonal and textual. Among the three, the interpersonal function is perhaps more relevant to this study as it concerns the relation between language and its users. Halliday says that "in interpersonal function the speaker is using the language as the means of his own intrusion into the speech event; the expression of his comments, his attitudes and evaluations, and also of the relationship that he sets up between himself and the listener."

(1973, 106) Therefore, the interpersonal function combines two categories, the effective and emotive function (communicating the speaker's attitudes) and the directive function (influencing the behaviour and the attitudes of the hearer. He further states that his model is "significant in literature since personality is dependent on interaction which is in turn mediated through language, the 'interpersonal' function in literature is both interactional and personal"as it expresses both the "inner and outer surfaces of the individual" (107).

Thus, in a linguistic study, the literary uses of language are placed against the background of more 'ordinary' uses of language, so that the poet or the novelist is seen using the same code, the same set of communicative resources.

Literature is said to be the most difficult type of language for stylistic observation because of the many complexities that appear in the course of examining the language. However, the study of literary texts which the linguists undertake from time to time shows that literary stylistics is a viable study. Literature contains a great deal of what is described as 'common core' although it does contain special or deviant features more than the non-literary texts. Literary style is marked by a careful and consistent use of regular patterns of language.

The language of literature appears more striking especially when the writer makes use of the resources available to all native speakers. Moreover, literary language is more formal and conscious but not spontaneous. Both poetry and prose are examples of a careful and often unexpected selection of words and syntactic constructions. However deviant the literary style may be, it cannot deviate too far from the expectation of speech community as it needs the vast readership.

The recent investigations of literary style show that literature acquires its real strength from the 'common core' and its deviations do not break down communication with common core users. One of the important tasks of literary stylistics is to determine how far and in what respects, a writer's language shows deviant features and how a writer uses generally accepted features for special effects. Furthermore, a writer does not restrict himself to one single register for the whole of his literary output. Therefore, the aim of literary stylistics is to recognise and examine the different registers in a given literary text.

Widdowson's (1975) contention is that stylistics is the study of literary discourse from a linguistic orientation and what distinguishes stylistics from literary criticism is that it is essentially a means of linking the two and it has no autonomous domain of its own. He shows that stylistics can provide a way of mediating between the two subjects: language and literature. The relationship is shown as follows:

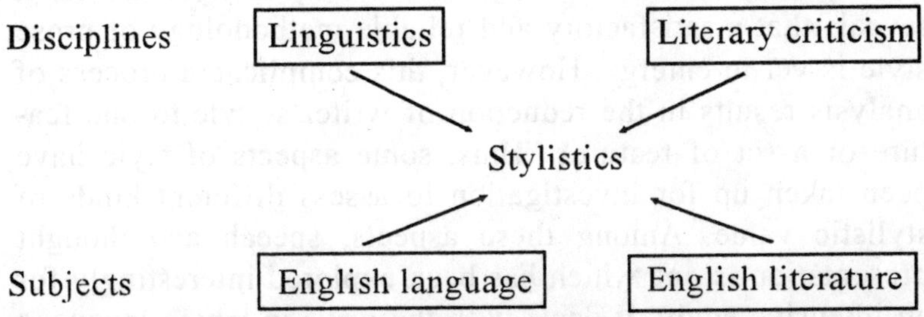

This diagram shows that "stylistics is neither a discipline nor a subject in its own right but a means of relating disciplines and subjects" (1975, 4).

For the modern linguist, the objective of examining the language of a literary text is to have a fuller understanding of the meaning it conveys and to appreciate the writer's artistic achievement. The literary text, therefore, is studied more for the meaning and its significance in the context.

But, for the linguist, the challenge of analysing prose style is greater than that of poetry. Poetry lends itself more easily to linguistic analysis than the novel, because aesthetic effect cannot be separated from manipulation of linguistic choices in poetry. On the other hand, in a novel, it (this effect) tends to depend on other factors such as character, theme and argument, and language is consciously used to achieve this effect. Linguistic techniques are easily applicable to a poem than to a full-scale novel. In a novel, the problem of what passages to select and what features to study has become serious and difficult. As a result, even the most detailed analysis looks incomplete. Perhaps that is why Spitzer (1949: 27) suggested that "the only way out of this state of unproductivity is to read and re-read." Edward Corbett, recommended the laborious method of copying out the whole text as a preliminary to analysing style. Ian Watt while analysing Henry James' style, admitted that he was "virtually helpless . . . . as far as fully developed and acceptable technique of explicating prose is concerned." (1981, 3) This major difficulty which has impeded the study of style in fiction reveals that a satisfactory and reliable methodology of prose style is yet to emerge. However, this complicated process of analysis results in the reduction of writer's style to one feature or a set of features. Thus, some aspects of style have been taken up for investigation to assess different kinds of stylistic value. Among these aspects, speech and thought presentation is one which has been explored interestingly for an intensive study. It deals with the ways in which language represents fiction through the relationship between the narrator and the reader. More precisely, it is concerned with the literary discourse of fictional characters. This book examines the speech and thought presentation techniques employed by Graham Greene in three novels: *The Power and the Glory, The Heart of the Matter* and *Doctor Fischer of Geneva or The Bomb Party*.

The study is organised as follows: The first chapter deals with the meaning and purpose of style and stylistics and how the problems of analysing prose style have prompted the linguist to direct his attention to the pragmatic aspect of language. A comprehensive summary of Searle's Speech Act theory (1969) and Grice's conversational implicature (1975) is attempted in this chapter.

The Second Chapter begins with a discussion of the discourse situation of the novel and the categories of narrative method. There is a discussion on the role and significance of speech/dialogue and its impact on the other elements in the novel such as characterization, narration, description etc.

The third chapter is divided into two parts. Part one examines various modes of speech presentation available to the novelist such as Direct Speech (DS), Indirect Speech (IS), Free Direct Speech (FDS), Free Indirect Speech (FIS) and the Narrative Report of Speech Act (NRSA). Part I ends with adopting the framework suggested by Leech and Short (1981) for analysing the three novels of Graham Greene.

Chapter four analyses the important modes of thought, presented by Greene in the three novels and how they are effective in the interest of character portrayal. This analysis precedes a brief description of different modes of thought viz., Direct Thought (DT), Free Direct Thought (FDT), Free Indirect Thought (FIT) and Narrative Report of Thought Act (NRTA) and how they are distinct from speech modes.

In the fifth chapter my attempt is first to explore the specific purposes of the author in employing various speech presentation techniques in his novels. Secondly to review the analysis for its pedagogic implications to the teachers as well as the students of literature in appreciating a literary work.

In the sixth chapter, the focus is on different kinds of points of view employed by Greene in his novels. They are (1) Spatio-temporal point of view (2) Ideological point of view and (3) Psychological point of view.

Since the purpose of this book is more practical than theoretical I have placed my emphasis on the study of several textual illustrations of Graham Greene. Incidentally, some of them are drawn from other important novelists' works, analysed by writers such as Geoffrey Leech, Mike Short and Norman Page. This book concludes with a summary on the effects produced by Greene through his stylistic strategies and how this analysis creates an awareness in the learner in his understanding of any literary writing.

WORKS CITED

Halliday, M.A.K. *Explorations in the Functions of Language* (London: Edward Arnold, 1973).

Leech, G.N.and Michael H. Short, *Style in Fiction. A Linguistic Introduction to English Fictional Prose* (English Language Series 13; London: Longman, 1981).

Widdowson, H.G. *Stylistics and the Teaching of Literature* (London: Longman, 1973).

CHAPTER 1

Developments in Narrative Style

In its general sense, the word style is the use of language in a given context by a given person. In the field of literature, the term style has been expanded to describe the linguistic habits of a particular writer (the style of Greene, Jane Austen etc.). Sometimes, it has been applied to the language used in a particular genre or period. For example, epistolary style, the style of Victorian novels etc. However, in this book we are concerned with authorial style.

Traditionally speaking, there is an intimate connection between style and an author's personality. Each writer has a 'linguistic thumb print,' a combination of linguistic expressions which are seen in his or her writing. But at the same time it cannot be denied that a writer's style is largely dependent on the subject matter he chooses or any extra linguistic factors which make his style distinctive from that of others. Even a writer like Samuel Johnson whose personality is reflected in all that he writes shows a great difference between the 'didactic and expository' prose of the essays in *The Rambler* and the simple narrative prose of *Rasselas*. Hence, it is difficult to generalise about an author's style. However, it is only the literary text that reveals the writer's style and lends itself to linguistic scrutiny. A text or an extract from a text is the nearest we can get to a homogeneous and specific use of language. In a text, it is possible to be more specific about how language serves a particular function which is the purpose of studying style. In other words, the goal of stylistics is to explain the relationship between language and artistic function. Further, stylistics provides descriptive frameworks by which the reader's hypothesis, concerning meaning and effects produced in texts can be explored through a systematic and principled attention to language.

The question from the linguist's point of view is, why the author has chosen to express his thoughts in a particular way whereas from the literary critic's point of view it is, how such an aesthetic effect has been achieved through language. So literary stylistics relates the critic's concern for appreciation to the linguist's concern for linguistic description. Thus, stylistics mediates between the disciplines of linguistics and literary criticism. It applies the methods and insights of linguistics to traditional problems that arise in literary analysis of language. Roger Fowler (1992, Vol. 4) and others prefer to call it 'critical linguistics.' In fact, linguistic observation stimulates or modifies literary insight and vice versa. Stylistics, being essentially evaluative, is an assessment of the effectiveness of linguistic choice. This choice depends on certain aesthetic intentions and constraints of means of expression. A stylistic analysis, therefore, depends upon the aesthetic judgement of the stylistician as well as the factors such as theoretical norms, stylistic categories and the context that surrounds the language.

Language critics such as Stanley Fist (1980) have criticised stylisticians for claiming too much for their readings and for using stylistic analysis as a mechanical procedure of discovery. But the claims made for stylistics are not as tendentious as critics have made out. The language of a literary text produces certain effects which aid to the reader's intuitive response to it. The purpose of stylistics is to formalize such intuitions, put them to test and then modify and refine them. Thus stylistics has made substantial contribution to persistent problems in the analysis of literary style (International Encyclopedia of Linguistics: 1992, Vol. 4).

1.1 Prose Style

For past twenty years, since Spitzer's and Watt's articles appeared (cf. Introduction), important developments have taken place in the linguistic study of prose style. Linguistics has become a more comprehensive discipline where the study of language is related to the conceptualization and communication of meaning. Language has been studied from different perspectives. The sociological and philosophical approaches to language and their application to literature have been particularly explored. The focus is more on the practical study of literary language.

There is no single model, applicable to linguistic research. The model of Transformational grammar which stresses the formal and cognitive aspects of language and which has dominated linguistic thinking for about fifteen years has been challenged by various models. The models which emphasize the social role and functional aspect of language have become significant.

The functional model, followed by linguists like Halliday and others (cf. Introduction), has directed its attention to the communicative and socially expressive functions of language. Similarly, the works of philosophers like Searle (speech act theory) and Grice (Conversational implicature) have influenced the researchers to shift their focus of linguistics to the communicative aspect of language.

The communicative aspect of language thus leads us to pragmatics to examine its role in the analysis of prose style.

1.2 A Pragmatic Approach to Language

According to Leech and Short, "The pragmatic analysis of language can be broadly understood to be the investigation into that aspect of meaning which is derived not from the formal properties of words and constructions but from the way in which utterances are used and how they relate to the context in which they are uttered." (1981, 290) In other words, in interpreting conversation in the novel, mere understanding of syntactic and lexical structures of utterances does not always help. An utterance should be studied in relation to its context. To demonstrate this, the pragmatic interpretative strategy, Leech and Short (1981) analyse an example from the novel *The Magus* by John Fowles. It is a short dialogue between the two characters Nicholas Urfe and Mr. Conchis.

> 'I shall see you next spring then?'
> 'Perhaps.'
> 'I have a two year contract at the school.'
> 'Ah . . .
> '. . . will she be here next year?'
> 'You will not see her.'
> 'But will she be here?'

In this conversation, Nicholas asks questions and Mr. Conchis replies. But there is an undercurrent to the conversation which can be understood by both the reader and the characters involved in the conversation. It may be observed that Conchis never gives straight-forward answers. At the beginning, Nicholas expects confirmation of his statement which is shown in his declarative form of first question. But Conchis' reply is totally neutral. Yet, Nicholas supports his statement by saying that he will be on the island for two years and thus indicates that they are likely to meet again. Conchis does not reply at all but merely says 'Ah' which means that he has understood. Later on, Conchis' reply is totally evasive when Nicholas asks him whether the girl he knows as Julie will be there. If she will not be there, it means naturally that he will not see her. But it is implied in the conversation that the fact that Nicholas will not see her again is not because of her not being there. Nicholas obviously realises this when he repeats his question 'But will she be here?' The repeated pattern allows Nicholas as well as the reader to deduce the meaning that Nicholas cannot be sure of meeting either Conchis or the girl again. "Throughout the novel, Nicholas repeatedly tries in vain to follow the two mysterious characters and thus this conversation exemplifies such major thematic preoccupation in the novel." (289-90).

This situation from *The Magus* can be similar to any real life situation. But the value given to Conchis' remarks cannot be arrived at merely through lexical and syntactic understanding of the text. So in order to understand the interaction between one character and the other, it is necessary and at the same time useful to apply some of the techniques used by those linguists who have developed pragmatic analysis.

In this chapter, a detailed study of the origin and development of pragmatics has been made.

1.3 Pragmatics as a Branch of Linguistics

Pragmatics is described as the study of the meaning of linguistic utterances for their users and interpreters. Charles Morris (1938), an American philosopher, distinguished it as a part of a major study called Semiotics, which is the study of signs and sign systems, from the other two parts being syntax and semantics. According to this line of thought, pragmatics is the study of signs in relation to their users. Syntax is the study of signs in relation to one another, whereas semantics is the study of signs in relation to what they refer to (Leech and Thomas, 1990, 173).

The purpose of pragmatics is not only to formalise the relation between symbols and what they represent in actual context but also to study the attitudes, behaviour and beliefs of symbol users. In fact, the latter is the main concern of pragmatics. For a long time, pragmatics was treated as insignificant and unimportant by philosophers and logicians like Rudolph Carnap. But later in the 1970s, the three philosophers—J.L. Austin, J.R. Searle and H.P. Grice became the inspirational sources for linguistic pragmatics. All three belonged to the ordinary language school of philosophy rather than the 'formal language' school represented by Carnap and others. They concentrated on how language conveys meaning and promotes the understanding of thought, logic and communication. They used the term 'communication' to associate language with its use to convey messages by users for interpreters and this is the heart of pragmatics.

Among them, the first philosopher J.L. Austin in his book, How to do things with words (1965), explored 'performative' utterances in language. He argued that utterances like

'I resign'
'I hereby give you notice of dismissal'

are problematic because although they have all the necessary qualities (signs) of being declarative sentences, their nature was 'performative' rather than constative in that their meaning was to be understood by the performance of an action. Thus in saying 'I resign' a person does the action i.e., resigns. Similarly, in saying 'I give notice' a person actually performs the action of giving notice. Austin stated that the conditions under which such utterances work are not truth conditions but rather felicity conditions or conditions of appropriateness.

Austin's further investigations led him to conclude that not only performative but all utterances can be explained in terms of actions. One could bring out the action like qualities of a statement, a question, a request etc., by prefixing an implicit performative to it. For example, the statement 'You'll be certainly paid tomorrow' has the underlying meaning 'I promise you that you'll be paid tomorrow.' In positing such a theory, Austin's claim is that linguistic phenomena are basically actions or deeds and an invitation to go beyond the traditional logician's limited concern with declarative or 'propositional' meaning.

He further extends this idea by saying that any utterance at the same time constitutes three kinds of act.

1. **Locutionary Act** (or locution) is the act of expressing something with a particular reference, e.g., He said to me "Shoot her."
2. **Illocutionary Act** (or illocution) is an act by the perfor-

mance of locution such as a request, an invitation etc., e.g., He urged or requested or invited me to shoot her.

3. **Perlocutionary Act** (or perlocution) is the act performed by means of what is said, e.g. He persuaded me to shoot her.

Austin's focus was on the second of these; the illocutionary act theory which is now considered as the territory of pragmatics, of meaning in context. The verbs used to describe illocutions such as claim, promise, beg, request, thank etc., can generally be used as performative verbs. Austin called the performative prefix 'I promise you . . . as an illocutionary force indicating device or IFID (1965, 101-3).

1.3.1 Speech Act Theory

After Austin, Searle's book Speech Acts (1969, 66-67) focuses on illocutionary acts and illocutionary force (concerns the functions or meanings associated with illocutionary acts). He offered certain important conditions in the lines of Austin's felicity conditions. According to him these conditions are necessary for a speech act to be effectively performed. They are as follows:

a) **Propositional Content Rules**: They specify the meaning expressed by the propositional part of an utterance. For instance, a promise refers to some future act by the speaker.

c) **Preparatory Rules**: They are the prerequisite conditions to the performance of speech act. For example, if an act of thanking is to be performed, the speaker must know that the hearer or addressee has done something of benefit to the speaker.

c) **Sincerity Rules**: They are the conditions to the act which has to be performed sincerely. For instance, if the act of an apology is to be sincere, the speaker must be sorry for what has been done.

d) **Essential Rules**: If a warning is to be performed it must fulfill the essential conditions, i.e., it counts as an undertaking that some future event is not in the interest of the addressee.

By positing these conditions, Searle argued that with these four rule types various speech acts can easily be distinguished.

The descriptive force of these conditions can be explained with the help of examples where these rules are violated. For instance, a request would be infelicitous if it did not refer to a future act (propositional content rules are violated).

> 'Could you please phone me last Monday?'

or if the hearer is asked to do something which he is not able to do.

> 'Would you mind translating this letter into French?' (spoken to someone who does not know French) (violation of preparatory rules).

Thus there is 'something odd' about these utterances if the conditions are violated.

Speech act theory led to the classification of illocutions. The multitude of different speech acts are reduced to an order and it was Searle who divided speech acts basically into five categories (1979, 12-20).

1) Assertives make the speaker commit to some kind of truth, e.g., declaring, stating, claiming, reporting, announcing etc.
2) Directives are the attempts to bring about some effect in the action of the hearer, e.g., requesting, ordering, begging, demanding etc.
3) Commissives make the speaker commit to some future

action, e.g., promising, offering etc.

4) Expressives are the expressions of some psychological state, e.g., thanking, apologising, congratulating etc.
5) Declarations are the speech acts that indicate the actual performance of some action, e.g., naming a ship, resigning, sentencing, dismissing, christening etc.

1.3.2 Conversational Maxims

The third philosopher in the group is H.P. Grice (Leech and Thomas 1990) who attempted to explain the difference between what is said and what is meant. What is said is what the words meant at the face value. What is meant is the effect that the speaker intends to produce on the addressee through his (addressee's) recognition of the speaker's intention. There is a considerable gap between these two kinds of messages—one consists of the explicit meaning while the other consists of implicit meaning. This can be understood by the following example.

> A: Where is Jane?
> B: Oh, she was walking in the direction of the bank ten minutes ago.

B's reply simply explains the behaviour of Jane 'ten minutes ago,' but by implication it suggests that the bank would be a good place to look for her. The implication is conveyed through shared contextual knowledge. It means that B expects A to share knowledge of the location of the particular bank he is referring to. But according to Grice even these assumptions do not explain the process of inferring conversational meanings entirely. Hence, he posited a rule called 'The co-operative principle' (CP) which states: "Make your contributions such as is required at the stage at which it occurs by the accepted purpose of direction of the talk exchange in which you are engaged." (Grice, 1975, 41-58)

The CP is expanded into four maxims:

a) The maxim of quality: It asserts: (i) try to make your contribution one that is true (ii) do not say what you believe to be false (iii) do not say that for which you lack adequate evidence.
b) The maxim of quantity specifies: i) make your contribution as informative as is required for the current purposes of the exchange (ii) do not make your contribution more informative than is required.
c) The maxim of relation says: make your contribution relevant.
d) The maxim of manner says: (i) be specific (ii) avoid obscurity (iii) avoid ambiguity (iv) be brief and orderly.

The above dialogue can be explained in terms of these maxims as follows: B's reply is not an answer to A's question at face value. But the maxim of relation leads A to expect that B is being relevant. The maxim of quality and quantity lead A to expect that what B says will give the right information to answer his question.

On the basis of this argument as well as from 'contextually shared knowledge' it is possible for A to infer that B does not know where Jane is but suggested that she may be at or near the bank. Hence, by CP, A can assume that it is B's intention to convey this implicit message. So it is possible to read extra meaning into what people say with the assumption that people not only know the meaning of expressions in their language but have general knowledge and general human rationality.

1.3.3 Conversational Implicature

However, Grice's CP is contradicted and criticised by many linguists like Apostel (1986), Kasher (1976) and Sampson (1982) who argued that it is simply a device to explain how people arrive at meanings, for, there is no evidence that people are inevitably truthful, informative and relevant in what they say (Leech and Thomas 1990). But Grice had already thought about this problem. Hence, he suggests the possibility of 'opting out' of the CP. For example, the utterance 'no comment' makes the hearer simply withhold whatever information he possesses. The other alternatives he has at his disposal are: (1) he can secretly violate a maxim—e.g., B could maliciously tell and mislead A by answering that Jane had walked in the opposite direction from the bank. (2) More importantly he can make a blatant show of breaking one of the maxims (in Grice's term, 'flouting a maxim') in order to make the hearer look for an implied meaning. According to Grice this is 'conversational implicature.' 'Conversational implicature' is a pragmatic implication which the hearer is able to understand by assuming the speaker's underlying adherence to CP. But the actual utterance of the speaker is the 'blatancy of the flouting of the maxim.' The following are examples of conversational implicatures (Leech and Thomas 1990, 182).

Flouting or violating the maxim of quantity:

> At the time of recording all the members of the cast were members of the BBC players.
> (Implicature: one or more of them are no longer members of the BBC players).

the maxim of manner

> Interviewer: Did the U.S. Govt. play any part in Duvalier's departure?
> Spokesman: I would not try to steer you away from that conclusion.
> (Implicature: The U.S. Govt. did play a role although the speaker does not wish to commit himself to the statement).

the maxim of relation

A: Has the doctor been?
Basil: What can I get you to drink?
A: Basil, has the doctor been?
Basil: Nuts?
(Implicature: Basil does not want to answer the question)

In this book, there is an attempt to apply Gricean principles to the fictional speech of Graham Greene.

Commenting on Grice's maxims, Levinson in his article "Activity types and language" (quoted by Leech and Thomas) says: "Grice's maxims of quality, quantity, relevance and manner are supposed to outline preconditions for the rational cooperative exchange of talk. But one thing we can observe is that not all activity types are deeply cooperative. Consider an interrogation: It is unlikely that either party assumes the other is fulfilling the maxims of quality, manner and especially quantity" (1990, 183).

However, as Leech and Thomas observe "the notion of implicature has been Grice's most important contribution to the development of pragmatics" (1990, 183). They assert that it is significant because unlike the material implication and entailment which can be defined in truth conditional terms, conversational implicature depends on factors of context.

WORKS CITED

Austin, J.L. *How to do things with words,* ed. J.O. Urmson (New York: OUP, 1965).

Bright, William, ed., *International Encyclopedia of Linguistics,* Vol. 4 (New York: OUP, 1992).

Fish, Stanley. *Is there a text in the class? The authority of interpretative communities* (Cambridge, Mass: HUP, 1980).

Grice, H.P. "Logic and Conversation" in *Syntax and Semantics: Speech Acts*, Vol. 3, ed. Cole Peter and J.L. Morgan (New York: Academics Press, 1975).

Leech, G.N. and H. Michael Short. *Style in Fiction: A Linguistic Introduction to English Fictional Prose* (ELS) (London: Longman, 1981).

Leech, G.N. and Jenny Thomas, "Language Meaning and Context: Pragmatics" in *An Encyclopedia of Language,* ed. N.E. Collinge (London, New York: Routledge, 1990).

Searle, J.R. *Speech Acts* (CUP, 1969).

CHAPTER 2

The Role of Speech in the Novel

2.1 The Novel as a Discourse

Unlike in spoken discourse, where one person conveys message to another for various purposes, the written discourse, such as a novel, has one addresser and a large number of unknown addressees. Literature is a kind of discourse where the writer is ignorant of the receiver, of his message or the situation in which it will be received. However, common knowledge and experience connect the author to the reader. Wayne C. Booth (1961, 138-39) calls this reader 'the implied reader.' The implied reader is one who shares with the author the general background knowledge of the world, a set of presuppositions, sympathies and standards of good and bad and right and wrong.

Just as there is the 'implied reader' between the reader and the work of fiction, Booth has observed an 'implied author' between the author and the text. 'The implied author' is referred as the author's 'second self.' Booth says, "even the novel in which no narrator is dramatized creates an implicit picture of an author who stands behind the scenes, whether as stage manager, as puppeteer, or an indifferent God, silently paring his fingernails." (1961, 151). Otherwise, the reader tends to attribute all the views and ideologies expressed through a work to the author himself. Authors may very often believe the views they are putting forward, but they need not. Generally, in a normal situation where there is no external evidence of the author's view, it is unreasonable to attribute the ideas expressed in the work of fiction to him. Similarly, the author cannot assume that the reader would respond and react to his message. Thus, the literary message does not 'take effect' in the way the non-literary message does. As Henry Widdowson rightly puts it

> . . . a piece of literary discourse is in suspense from the usual process of social interaction whereby senders address message directly to receivers. The literary message does not arise in the normal course of social activity as do other messages, it arises from no previous situation and requires no response, it does not serve as a link between people or as a means of furthering the business of ordinary social life. (1975, 51)

Thus, in the discourse of a novel, whether it is indirect or embedded, the message being totally disengaged from an immediate situational context, is communicated to an addressee who cannot respond.

The discourse of a novel is presented in different methods of narration which make a crucial distinction between the author and the narrator.

2.2 The Types of Narrative Method

Critics visualise mainly three categories of narrative method. They are (1) the omniscient narrator method (2) the autobiographical or I-narrator method and (3) epistolary method. The first two are considered significant by most of the novelists and hence they are discussed here.

2.2.1 The Omniscient Narrator Method

In the early nineteenth century, the third person narrative method was considered 'disagreeable' or a 'defect in a work of fiction' where authorial intrusion is dominant. But, later on, this method received more attention from critics like Leslie Stephen, quoted by Kenneth Graham (1965, 123), who stated "we are indeed told dogmatically that a novelist should never indulge in little asides to the reader. Why not? One main advantage of a novelist as it seems to me is precisely that it leaves room for a freedom in such matters which is incompatible with the requirement, for example of dramatic writing."

The main advantage of third person narration is that the narration is presented to the reader directly without an intermediary. The absence of I enables the reader to understand that the 'implied author' and the narrator are one and the same. It is for this reason that most third person narrators are for the purpose of fiction, omniscient.

2.2.2. I-Narrator Method

The autobiographical method or the I-narrator method makes a crucial distinction between the author and the narrator, and the narrator may well be talking to someone distinct from the reader. The choice of first person narration where 'I' is also a primary character in the story, establishes a personal relationship with the reader and wins his favour towards the character-narrator. This device may even convert certain views of the reader which he would not normally hold for the duration of the story. Therefore, the need to postulate an 'implied reader' has arisen.

According to Leech and Short (1981, 269), a novel can contain four levels of discourse embedded one inside another operating at the levels of (a) author and reader (b) implied author and reader (c) narrator and interlocutor and finally (d) character and character as shown in the figure.

Addresser I ————> Message —————> Addressee I
(author) (reader)
Addresser II ————> Message —————> Addressee II
(implied author) (implied reader)

Addresser III ————> Message ————> Addressee III
(narrator) (interlocutor)
Addresser IV ————> Message ————> Addressee IV
(character) (character)

My attempt in this book is to penetrate the most deeply embedded level of discourse where character talks to character (level 4) and where messages can move in either direction. Now this leads us to the examination of the role of 'character talk' or dialogue in the novel.

2.3 Dialogue in the Novel

The general assumption is that the main task of the novel is to represent life in its rich detailed circumstantiality. Readers take it for granted that English novelists have been concerned to hold up the mirror to reality. This is evident in formal criticism of fiction as well as the reaction of the reader. In fact, to speak of a novel 'mirroring life' is indeed seriously misleading in relation to the question of style. Unlike as in life, in literary work every word is selectively and purposefully employed. In fiction, nothing can be dismissed as irrelevant. Action, description and speech are strictly finite as against the reality where they are unselected and unlimited.

Hence, the language of a novel has a density and meaningfulness which bears a degree of scrutiny that is not always seen in the discourse of everyday life. This point is established by Mark Schorer.

> As for the resources of language, these somehow we almost never think of as part of the technique of fiction—language as used to create a certain texture and tone which in themselves state and define themes and meanings; or language, the contents of ordinary speech, as forced, through conscious manipulation into all those larger meanings which our ordinary speech almost never intends. (1972, 387-88)

Walter Allen states, "like any other artist, the novelist is a maker. He is making an imitation, an imitation of the life of man on earth. He is making, it might be said, a working model of life as he sees and feels it" (1958, 14). If the novel imitates life, then this must be taken as an account of its effects rather than of its methods. But paradoxically novelists have discovered that the quality of life can be most successfully evoked by exploiting conventions of prose fiction rather than by faithful adherence to reality.

Speech has a distinctive role in the creation of illusion in a novel. It is this element that comes closest to reality because in the presentation of speech, the author's presence becomes unobtrusive. Narrative, description and comment are familiar literary modes. But dialogue plays an important role in life, both outside and inside novels. It is obvious that in a novel, dialogue helps to develop plot and enriches the reader's understanding of character and background. At the same time, it creates a distinctive and intrinsic interest which no other manner of presentation could. In reading fictional dialogue the illusion of listening to the conversation of those in real life is created. Thus, the dialogue in a novel echoes the accepted speech of the day.

However, the concept of realism when applied to fictional speech is often based on an inadequate or inaccurate notion of spontaneous speech. Knowledge of structural features and distinguishing and multitudinous varieties of actual speech is still inadequate. As a result, fictional speech has been branded as non-realistic and conventional. However, spoken language continues to be a norm against which dialogue may be judged.

Norman Page (1973) rightly states that no dialogue in a novel is an accurate transcript of actual speech. He gives three important reasons for this. In the first place, the normal characteristics of spoken language though perfectly tolerable in the spoken form would be quite unacceptable in the written medium. An accurate transcript of any spontaneous speech clarifies this. Its hesitations and repetitions, its silence fillers, its grammatical inconsistencies and incompleteness are all distinct from fictional speech. For instance, Randolph Quirk has quoted from transcripts of the recorded speech of University graduates in English.

> he—seemed of course he had that kind of er I I'm er I I er I I er er are you northern by any chance. I was going to say that kind of northern—er scepticism or at least questioning mind—which er—but of course he would mislead you with that he er he gave you the impression that the only er you know he gave you the impression that he was—sceptical and at times sceptical and nothings else. (1972, 6-7)

A passage like this provides real speech but no novelist is likely to use it in his novel in the name of a dialogue. Language 'chopped and gurgled' in this way is generally described and not precisely rendered unless for a specific purpose.

Secondly, in real life, speech derives much of its significance from the context. But in a novel the extra linguistic referents must be rendered consciously and explicitly by linguistic means alone. The fictional speaker cannot share the given elements which are enjoyed by the speaker in real life unconsciously. Thus the novelist has no shared context available which he can take for granted. But it must be produced within the text of the novel. As a result, fictional dialogue is more 'heavily burdened' with informative and suggestive detail than the speech of everyday life. However, as Norman Page asserts, this explicitness in providing the contextual elements within the text may deprive fictional dialogue of some of the 'subtlety and meaningful ambiguity' of actual speech situation. But it ensures clarity and precision that renders literary dialogue essentially different from everyday talk. Dialogue then becomes 'explanatory, self-contained, sharper and surer in its effects and therefore more memorable' (1973, 8-9).

Thirdly in spoken dialogue, most of the information is conveyed by the phonological component which written language is ill-equipped to convey. It is often difficult to convey such meaningful features of speech as pause, stress and intonation through writing. The fact is that the finite set of an alphabet cannot fully represent the infinite variety of speech. However, this has not deterred writers from trying to do their best with the limited means at their disposal. For instance, variant spellings have been widely employed by novelists from the eighteenth century onwards to represent the non-standard pronunciation. But these are only partial solutions. As Mark Twain wrote (quoted by J.C. Gerber, 1959, quoted by N. Page, 1973, 10) in one of his letters "the moment talk is put into print you recognize that it is not what it was when you heard it; you perceive that an immense something has disappeared from it." So the novelist who aims at producing a sense of the spoken language is concerned with recapturing this 'immense something,' and whether he is fully successful in his attempt is doubtful.

In order to be realistic the novelist has to establish a delicate balance between the use of some of the features of actual speech and the code of stylistic conventions employed by him. Hemingway's dialogue has been praised for giving an 'illusion of reality that reality itself would not give.' Such praise is a tribute to the writer's success in performing the balancing act. If he is more conventional the dialogue would be rejected as literary and artificial. On the other hand, if he is less conventional it would lose in sharpness and accuracy. Dialogue which is too close to actual speech becomes wearisome and irritating. But speech that is too remote from real life hurts the reader's sense of reality.

The importance of dialogue in relation to other elements in a literary work varies a good deal from one novel to another and between different parts of the same novel. The novelist, unlike the dramatist is at liberty to combine speech with narration and description in variable proportion. This liberty places the responsibility on the novelist to select the most appropriate mode or combination of modes for a particular passage, scene or episode in the novel and this calls for stylistic variety to be employed by him in the novel. Thus, the presentation of speech in the novel by the author depends on the stylistic relationship existing between dialogue and non-dialogue passage.

Although dialogue will often serve to advance plot, certain writers like Jane Austen use it to contribute to the presentation and development of characters. Many writers tend to differentiate between the speech of their major characters to ensure clarity and variety. Thus speech becomes a 'badge of identity' and a way of enriching the reader's awareness of a given character's individuality. Indeed the experience of repeatedly encountering well-known voices is one of the ways in which the sense of a distinctive world is created. For instance, Joseph Andrews in Fielding's novel, Miss Bates and Mrs. Elton in Jane Austen's *Emma*, doctor Fischer in Greene's *Doctor Fischer of Geneva* are all individualised substantially through their speech.

Character individualization through dialogue is based on observable facts of life. But sometimes, they tend to go beyond the real in the novel. In real life, judgements or misjudgements about a character are constantly made on the basis of speech characteristics. In fiction, the novelist invites the reader to do this more confidently since the evidence is 'planted' in the dialogue with a set purpose.

Many questions are raised regarding the place of dialogue in a novel in relation to other elements. This is because the novelist cannot avoid continually exercising a choice between different modes of presentation. For instance, in introducing a character, in rendering of a dramatic episode or in presenting some necessary information he has to choose between dialogue and narrative or descriptive prose of a combination of these. If he decides to make use of dialogue, a further selection of speech presentation has to be made. Therefore, any novel may raise the question whether speech habitually carries the main burden of fiction or whether it is partly performed by other means. The more specifically stylistic question that may be raised is, what kind of linguistic differences exist between dialogue and non-dialogue writing.

WORKS CITED

Allen, Walter. *The English Novel* (London: Phoenix House, 1954).

Booth, Wayne C. *The Rhetoric of Fiction* (Chicago: University of Chicago Press, 1961).

Graham, Kenneth. *English Criticism of the Novel. 1865-1900* (London: OUP, 165).

Page, Norman. *Speech in the English Novel*, ELS (London: Longman, 1973).

Schorer, Mark. "Technique as Discovery" in *20th Century Literary Criticism*, ed. David Lodge (London: Longman, 1972), pp. 387-88.

Widdowson, Henry G. *Stylistics and the Teaching of Literature* (London: Longman, 1975).

CHAPTER 3

The Presentation of Speech

PART I

Methods of Presenting Speech in a Novel

There are primarily, two ways of presenting speech: the direct and the indirect. However, a careful study of any novel reveals that these simple and clearly defined categories fail to accommodate many passages, especially in the work of writers from the eighteenth century onwards. There appears to be a need for both an adequate framework and terminology which describe and analyse the novels. Therefore, an in-depth and careful study of familiar and unfamiliar categories employed by the writers consciously or unconsciously in their novels is necessary.

Leech and Short, in *Style in Fiction*, exclusively deal with this subject in the last chapter. According to them (1981, 321-22), the modes of speech presentation available to novelists are: Direct Speech (DS), Indirect Speech (IS), Free Direct Speech (FDS), Free Indirect Speech (FIS) and the Narrative Report of Speech Act (NRSA). The attempt in this chapter is to discuss various uses and effects of these modes individually.

3.1.1 Direct Speech (DS)

There are, generally, three common conventions in the use of Direct Speech. One is, the custom of reproducing dialogue even in a first person narrative, accurately and completely without any reservations. The second convention is, that in which actual speech with its quotation marks and other graphological and typographical indications is recorded. The practice of using quotation marks in certain contexts which was prevalent until the beginning of the nineteenth century appears to be obsolete now. The following examples from Fielding and Dickens respectively illustrate this point (N. Page 1973, 29).

> Meeting the landlady, he accosted her with great civility, and asked "What he could have for dinner."

> He checks his horse and asks a workman does he know the name of Ronncewell thereabouts. (*Bleak House*, Ch. 6)

The second example shows a tendency towards the integration of direct speech with narrative style which I discuss later.

The third convention is that in which several separate speeches are conflated into single speech. Doctor Fischer's characteristic expressions of pride in the novel *Doctor Fischer of Geneva* is a good example of this.

> . . . perhaps the porridge will slow you down, Deane, my poor fellow. Albert, another plate for Mr. Kips and I see Mrs. Montgomery is nearly ready. Hurry up, Divisionnaire, hurry up Belmont. No presents before everyone has finished.
>
> . . . Bravo Divisionnaire. You are catching them up. You ply a good spoon, Deane, my boy, I wish your female admirers could see you at this moment, guzzling away. (60)

Here, Greene tries to present the cumulative effect of Doctor Fischer's egoistic addressing of his friends at the party. Therefore, his entire conversation is presented as a monologue in the interest of the character portrayed. The proud, cruel and contemptuous attitude of Doctor Fischer to his so-called friends is revealed in his conflated speech.

Therefore, direct speech is not a single method but ranges from the undoctored to the stylized. Its distinctive virtue lies in its capacity to allow a character to speak in an individual voice, directly to the reader without the presence of authorial intervention. Immediacy and the stylistic variety achieved in dialogue are seen as its advantages. The limitations of direct speech, on the other hand, are its tendency towards 'diffuse-ness and a consequent thinness of effect and the need for frequent gear-shifting from non-dialogue to dialogue elements and back again' (Norman Page, 1973, 31).

3.1.2 Indirect Speech (IS)

While direct speech reports what someone has said using the words verbatim, an indirect report expresses what is said in the narrator's own words. The difference is shown in the following examples (Leech and Short 1981, 319).

1) He said "I'll come back here to see you again tomorrow." (DS)
2) He said that he would return there to see her the following day. (IS)

The following rules will be applied to convert Direct Speech into Indirect Speech.

i) The inverted commas around the reported speech are removed making the reported speech dependent on the reporting verb.
ii) The subordinating conjunction 'that' is introduced to mark the dependence.
iii) First and second person pronouns are changed to third person.
iv) The present tense of the verb changes to past and the time adverb 'tomorrow' changes to the 'following day.' The deictic adverb 'here' is changed to 'there.'

In examples 1 and 2 the time and place for the reported and reporting speech events are totally different. But in some conversations, the extra linguistic referents will be the same for both primary and secondary speech situations. Then the relevant deictics can remain unchanged. For instance, if sentence 1 is uttered in a hospital and the person is reporting it in the same building on the same day, sentence 2 will be as follows:

3) He said that he would come back *here* to see her/you again *tomorrow*.

Here the pronoun 'you' will also remain unchanged in IS, if the addressee is identical in the two speech situations. Hence, we can conclude that the "mode of speech presentation is determined not only by the presence of formal linguistic features but also by our knowledge of extra linguistic, contextual factors" (1981, 320).

According to Meir Sternberg (1991), indirect speech or 'reported discourse is a mimesis of discourse by discourse' in the sense that—what the reporter says in the subject's name belongs to one discourse and the subject's actual words quoted belong to another. So it is 'discourse within discourse.' Thus, the discourse reported "becomes an inset within the frame of the reporting discourse, often with the help of an introductory clause or transformer" (63).

Sternberg further says that IS is "a communicative subordination of the part to the whole that encloses it. To quote is to re-contextualize, if not to re-textualize, hence to interfere with the original con(text) . . . all reporters in short, subject the original to their own rules, needs ends, indeed 'framing it in the process'" (*Literary Pragmatics* 1991, 64).

Gaining pace and economy by compensating for the loss of immediacy is seen as the main advantage of using indirect speech. It can also combine more readily with narrative style. It is said that although IS helps the writer employ a neutral style in the novel, it still represents individual varieties of speech. Sometimes, indirect speech is seen to possess features that belong to both the indirect form and the direct form. Hence, in analysing the novel, it is necessary to be aware of 'degrees of indirectness.' This is illustrated in the following passages (1973, 31).

1. Lydia was bid by her two eldest sisters to hold her tongue. . . . Turning to Mr. Bennet he [Mr. Collins] offered himself as his antagonist at backgammon. (Jane Austen, *Pride and Prejudice*, Ch. 14)
2. Mrs. Bickerton assured her, that the acceptance of any reckoning was entirely out of the question. (Scott, *The Heart of the Midlothian*, Ch. 28)
3. The doctor accused Mr. Allworthy of too great levity repeated his accusations against his brother, and declared that he should never more be brought either to see, or to own him for his relation. (Fielding, *Tom Jones*, Ch. 12)
4. Mr. Sapsea expressed his opinion that the case had a dark look; in short (and here his eyes rested full on Nelville's countenance), an un-english complexion. (Dickens, *Edwin Drood*, Ch. 15)
5. Mrs. O'dowd (described) how it had been presented to her by her father as she slipt into the car'ge after her mar'ge. (Thackeray, *Vanity Fair*, Ch. 28)

The question that arises from these examples is, to what extent can the original words be reconstructed by the indirect form?

The first example belongs to narrative style. It is not indirect speech that is presented here but what N. Page calls 'submerged speech.' Dialogue is absorbed by narrative with consequent changes in lexis as well as grammatical form. The second example belongs to 'traditional' indirect speech with back shifting. The combination of the two forms may be seen in the third example. The first half of Fielding's sentence indicates qualities of direct speech but the second half moves to indirect speech. The fourth example is different from the third in the sense that in its subordinate clause it shows features of direct speech ('dark look,' 'un-English complexion'). Therefore, in this case, indirect speech does not lose immediacy and vividness by not preventing the reader from hearing Sapsea in his individuality. It is called 'parallel indirect speech.' The indirect version of the last example involves not only syntactic and lexical but also phonological changes. In this case, the Anglo-Irish pronunciation of Mrs. O'dowd is given. So it is called 'coloured' or 'modified' indirect speech.

Thus, through these examples it is suggested that there are at least three degree of variation in the presentation of indirect speech. However, this analysis is contradicted by Leech and Short which will be discussed later in this book.

3.1.3. Free Indirect Speech (FIS)

Free Indirect Speech as its name implies is a freer version of the indirect form. Unlike in IS, in FIS the reporting clause is omitted but the selection of tense and pronoun follows the rules of IS. Accordingly, the free indirect versions of sentence 2 are as follows:

2a. He would return there to see her again the following day.
2b. He would return there to see her again tomorrow.
2c. He would come back there to see her again tomorrow.

(a) is an example of FIS because of the absence of the reporting clause. But the reported clause shares some of the syntactic features of the main clause that are associated with direct speech (DS). This is demonstrated in (b) and (c) which are successively freer versions of (a) because of the presence of near deictics 'tomorrow' in (b) and 'come back' and 'tomorrow' in (c). FIS has a peculiar status in terms of truth claims and faithfulness. Though it is not a reproduction of the original speech, it is certainly more than a 'mere indirect rendering of the original' (1981, 321).

Talking about Free Indirect Style, Sternberg (1991, 66) says that it has "managed to capture, almost to monopolize theoretical attention in a number of disciplines: linguistics, stylistics, poetics with its diversity of names such as Style indirect libre, erlebte Rede, quasi-direct Speech, narrated monologue."

The characteristic features of FIS as enumerated by S. Ullmann in his "Style in French Novel" (1957) quoted by N. Page (1973, 37) are:

1. Transposition of Verbs: As in indirect speech, if the narrative is in the past tense, the verbs will change, the present becoming preterite, the pluperfect etc. However, it is possible to find exception to this.
2. Transposition of Pronouns: Just as in indirect speech, first and second person change to third.
3. Absence of Subordination: Each sentence appears as an independent unit, not a subordinate clause, so that there is no key verb on which it is syntactically dependent.
4. Retention of 'Emotive Elements' such as questions, exclamations, interjections, colloquial language, slang and vulgar terms together with an attempt to initiate the 'inflection and intonations of the speaking voice.'

Though FIS is identified and discussed by the linguists of only the twentieth century, it was prevalent in the works of a number of writers of the nineteenth century.

To show the effects of FIS in the novel two examples are discussed here. The first one is the portrayal of the lawyer Mr. Shepherd's speech in 'persuasion' which is analysed by Leech and Short (1981, 326).

> "Then I take it for granted," óbserved Sir Walter 'that his face is about as orange as the cuffs and capes of my livery.' Mr. Shepherd hastened to assure him, that Admiral Croft was very hale, hearty, well-looking man, a little weather-beaten, to be sure, but not much; and quite

> the gentleman in all his notions and behaviour;—not likely to make the smallest difficulty about terms:—only wanted a comfortable home, and to get into it as soon as possible; knew he must pay for his convenience;—knew what a rent a ready furnished house of that consequence might fetch;—should not have been surprised if Sir Walter had asked more;—had inquired about the manor;—would be glad if the deputation, certainly but made no great point of it;—said he sometimes took out a gun but never killed;—quite the gentleman. (Chapter 3)

Sir Walter's speech is presented in the direct form. But Mr. Shepherd who plays a different role altogether is given the more 'self-effacing' indirect form of speech. Beginning in IS, his speech slips into FIS by virtue of the fact that the subordinating conjunction 'that' and the subject are not repeated. The colloquial lexical forms, dashes and the lawyer's repetition of the reassuring phrase 'quite the gentleman' indicate that only parts of the conversation are presented here. Thus FIS is shown as a form which is a blend of the speeches of the intervening narrator and the original speaker. The shortened statements of Mr. Shepherd's speech about the Admiral highlight the 'inexhaustibility of the lawyer's store of eager reassurances.' FIS creates an ironic distance between the reader and the character and the reader is made to realise that Mr. Shepherd's persuasiveness is for his own benefit rather than Sir Walter's. Thus FIS is used as an extremely useful technique for throwing ironic light on what the character says.

Unlike many writers on speech presentation, Leech and Short (1981) feel that no one particular feature has to be present for FIS to occur. As they themselves assert, their definition is one in terms of 'family resemblance' rather than one that depends upon the presence of a particular defining feature. By the term family resemblance they mean that these modes of speech presentation belong to the same family and so there are common features between any two modes. The main reason for this approach is "the occurrence of sentences which exhibit subordination but which would appear to belong to the semantic half-way house reserved for FIS" (1981, 330). The second example is from Paul Scott's *Staying On* which has been analysed by Leech and Short (1981) as evidence of their approach.

> He said he must persuade Billy-boy build a pod in the hotel compound one day when old Ma Bhoolaboy was out playing bridge so that when her Tonga brought her back at night the whole thing would tip in with a bloody great splash. (Ch. 11)

In this example, though subordination is present, colloquial forms like 'old Ma Bhoolaboy' and 'with a bloody great splash' indicate that in the subordinate clause it is not just an indirect report of the statement that is presented, but a flavour of the original words spoken by the character. Therefore, it may be observed that the sentence begins in the indirect mode and then slips into the free indirect form.

This analysis contradicts N. Page's suggestion that examples which show subordination but which also possess lexical or graphological features associated with DS belong to 'coloured indirect speech' (of 3.1.2). His assumption is that syntactic features alone determine the speech presentation category. But Leech and Short (1981, 331) argue that this approach ignores the fact that the 'claim to faithfulness' in examples like those discussed above (second example) is the same as that found in examples where subordination is absent (first example). Hence, it is asserted that features from any of the three major linguistic levels might be instrumental in indicating that a particular sentence is in FIS. Further, it is stated, that sometimes a single lexical or graphological features is enough to suggest that the sentence is in FIS which is exemplified in the following sentences.

He said that the bloody train had been late.
He told her to leave him alone!

In these examples the features that show that they are in FIS are the swear word in the first sentence and the exclamation mark in the second. Rarely are these forms used by novelists. Hence, they can be attributed to the character's manner of expression.

This version is taken as the basis for the study of Greene's fiction.

This kind of use of FIS is found in Fielding and in some non-literary texts written even earlier, because FIS allows immediacy and avoids continual repetition of the reported clause.

3.1.4 Free Direct Speech (FDS)

There are two features in DS which show the evidence of narrator's presence. They are 1) the quotation marks and 2) the introductory reporting clause. FDS is distinct from DS as it shows the absence of one or both of these features and thus produces a free form. In FDS, the characters speak directly without the narrator as an intermediary. For example, the development of FDS is shown in the following manner.

He said "I'll come back here to see you again tomorrow."
I'll come back here to see you again tomorrow.

Hemingway uses this technique in his novels. He omits the reporting clause even in long conversations and thus creates an ambiguity in the identification of the speakers in the dialogue. James Joyce on the other hand uses running speech and narrative together by omitting the inverted commas. He uses this technique to indicate that speech and narrative are two 'distinguishable aspects of one state.' Similarly, Dickens omits the quotation marks and locutionary clauses in his novel *Bleak House*. All these writers use FDS to create a kind of ambiguity in the conversation (1981). However Graham

Greene uses FDS to create different effects which will be discussed in part B.

3.1.5 Narrative Report of Speech Act (NRSA)

Another method of speech presentation is the Narrative Report of Speech Act. It is more "indirect than the indirect speech." Unlike in IS, in NRSA the narrator does not give the entire sense of what was stated. Hence the sentence 'he said I'll come back here to see you again tomorrow' can be reported in the following ways.

He promised to return.
He promised to visit here again.

In both these sentences the minimal account of the statement is given. Thus NRSA is used in the novels generally to summarize relatively unimportant stretches of conversation.

When a novelist reports the occurrence of some speech act, the reader views the things in the novel entirely from his point of view. But when the reader moves along the cline of speech presentation from the more controlled to the more free and (FDS) where the characters are left to talk on their own, the author's interference seems to be less noticeable.

The cline of 'interference' in report is illustrated by Leech and Short (1931, 324).

Narrator in total control of report	Narrator in partial control of report	Narrator not in control of report

Varieties of speech presentation

NRA NRSA IS FIS DS FDS

It is with reference to this framework of various modes of speech presentation, I attempt to analyse the three novels of Graham Greene.

PART II

The Presentation of Speech in Greene's Novels

The study of 'character speech' in the novel is significant because a major portion of most of the novels is in terms of conversation between characters. It is generally presented in direct speech and an understanding of 'character speech' is necessary for appreciating the content of the novel. This analysis of how characters communicate with each other also contributes to the development of the awareness of the one sided conversation between the author and the reader. Thus, a study of conversation leads to the pragmatic analysis of speech in the novel. The theory of pragmatic analysis of ordinary conversation is discussed in detail in Chapter 1. I feel a brief survey of pragmatic principles and conversational maxims is necessary before the analysis of fictional speech in the novels of Graham Greene.

In order to understand the interaction between characters in dialogue it will be useful to see how the conversational maxims proposed by Grice and Searle (cf. 1.3) are applicable to Greene's novels. First, it is necessary, therefore, to examine a speech act in an ordinary conversation which helps in understanding the pragmatic force of an utterance. The concept of speech act which is developed by J.L. Austin and J.R.Searle (cf. Ch. 1) is significant because it relates utterance meaning to context. Speech acts such as asking, requesting, declaring etc., have different syntactic and semantic forms. For example, the three different syntactic forms which are also semantically different in the following utterances may be considered.

Please write to him. (imperative)
Could you please write to him? (interrogative)
I'd like you to write to him. (declarative)

The first and third sentences have the same pragmatic force, because both the sentences express a sort of control over the hearer. Hence, the pragmatic force of an utterance and its semantic sense must be separated. Thus, we can observe, that pragmatics is "concerned with the enactment, through language of situational reality and in fact it is the function of an important class of elements called deictics (this, that, here, there, now, then, I, you, present and past tenses etc.) to refer directly or indirectly to elements of the situation." (1981, 291)

In pragmatics much of what is learnt is derived from inferences from the language but not from its overt sense. Generally, in a novel, utterances such as requests are not mere requests but have 'extra meanings' that the readers can infer. These extra meanings which 'account for a gap between overt sense and pragmatic force' are called implicatures (c.f. chapter 1). The conversational maxims, proposed by H.P. Grice (cf 1.3) unlike rules of grammar are often violated. An extract from *The Heart of the Matter* is examined to illustrate this point.

> 'Are you feeling better darling? Louise said, Mrs.Castel's been in.' 'Enough to make anyone ill,' Scobie said. 'She's been telling me about you.' 'What about me?' (part 1, ch. 1, 23)

In this conversation, Louise breaks the maxim of quantity and manner. She has not given an adequate answer to Scobie's question and so breaks the maxim of quantity. To a simple and straightforward question like 'are you feeling better,' 'yes' or 'no' would have been the shortest and uncomplicated answer. But Louise supplies additional information that is about Mrs. Castle's coming and thus breaks the maxim of manner. The reason for Louise breaking the maxim could be that she anticipates the next question by her husband to be the reason for her looking ill which is obviously understood by Scobie. Scobie reasonably concludes from his wife's answer that the news brought by Mrs. Castle has caused her illness. Hence, the rest of the conversation runs smoothly without either of them breaking any maxim. It may also be observed that the two characters are obeying the 'Co-operative Principle' even though the maxims are violated .

The interaction between Scobie and Yusef, the Syrian trader, offers another example from the same novel.

> 'It's an odd coincidence that you are here just at the moment when he commits suicide.'
> 'I think myself it is providence.'
> 'He owed my store-manager money.'
> 'What sort of pressure were you putting on him Yusef?'

Yusef's reply to Scobie's suspicious statement breaks the maxim of quantity as he attributes his presence 'there' to God's will. Yusef breaks both the maxim of quality and manner by making a false reply that the D.C. had owned money to his store-manager. Scobie seems to understand the implicature and asks a direct question this time after concluding that he had started putting pressure on the D.C. Though Yusef avoids direct replies to Scobie's queries, Scobie can see through the implicative force of his utterances and expresses his helplessness (since there is no evidence for his crime) as the passage goes further—'There's quite a lot in what you say Yusef.'

The interpretation of implicatures assumes that the Cooperative Principle is being obeyed. But sometimes the participants have a choice whether to cooperate or not. This is proved in the conversation between Mr. Jones and the insolent servant of Dr. Fischer in the novel *Doctor Fischer of Geneva*.

> 'Have you an appointment?'
> 'Yes.'
> 'What name?'
> 'Jones.'

'I don't know that he can see you.'
'I told you, I have an appointment.'
'Oh, appointments,' he said in a tone of disdain.
'Everyone says he has an appointment.' (26)

As is observed here, the servant wilfully breaks the Cooperative Principle by not believing what Jones says. In the earlier example it is found that Yusef is evasive and thus refuses to obey the Co-operative Principle. In both these cases the communication is not successful.

Two important points are illustrated in these three passages. The first one is that, although implicature can be seen as the basis of any ordinary conversation, the possibility of interpersonal factors such as attitude, tension and conflict making the speakers violate the Principle cannot be ruled out. The second point is that, the participant, in a conversation, constructs a 'model of context' which includes his relation with his interlocutor.

Implicatures are contributions made to this 'model' as the conversation proceeds, when characters are at cross purposes as in Doctor Fischer's passage the models are at variance. 'Such variance is the basis of dramatic interest in the conversational dialogue in the novel' (1981, 299).

3.2.1. Speech between the Author and the Reader

The pragmatic model of analysis also applies to the way in which authors convey messages to their readers, which is of course one sided. Moreover, it is assumed that adherence to the Cooperative Principle is greater than that of the day-to-day conversation because the writer has a good deal of time to choose exactly what he wants to say. This, he conveys sometimes through characters and sometimes directly, in both cases the conversational implicatures are expected to be used.

The author uses the generic present while conveying what he wishes to say. Thus, he breaks away from the narrative past maintaining relevance to the narrative. This relevance is clearly seen in *The Power and the Glory*, Part II, Chapter 1.

> It is one of the strange discoveries a man can make that life, however you lead it, contains moments of exhilaration; there are always comparisons which can be made with worse times; even in danger and misery the pendulum swings. (59)

After travelling through the forest for nearly twelve hours the priest and the mule get tired and the mule suddenly sits down. Seeing this, the priest begins to laugh. It is in this context that the above comment of general truth is made by the omniscient author. The implicature is direct in this case. The assumption is that comparing the present situation with worse times he has had, the priest might have felt some moments of happiness. The priest's happiness can also be attributed to the fact that driven by the presence of soldiers, he reached the village where he most wanted to be, and it is here that his child and her mother live.

Another example of generic comment by the author is found in *Doctor Fischer of Geneva*.

> But death, I was to argue later, annuls promises. A promise is made to a living person. A dead person is already not the same as the one who was alive. (64)

Jones is made to promise to Anna-Luise that he will never go back to Doctor Fischer's parties. But he breaks the promise after she dies. Here the implicature is that the I-narrator who breaks the maxim of quality justifies his violation in this statement that a promise is valid as long as the person is alive.

The reader is thus invited, in the novel, to draw implicatures both from the character's speech and authorial commentary. This kind of analysis explains and justifies the intuitive reactions of a reader to fictional dialogue.

So far the focus has been on the pragmatic model of understanding in relation to character-character and author reader speech in a novel which is presented in the direct form (DS) by the author. But the author has other modes of speech presentation, discussed earlier in general. The attempt here is to study the application of these modes to the novels of Graham Greene. One of the effective modes of presentation that the novelist has at his disposal is FDS.

3.3.2 The Presentation in FDS

Greene uses this mode of speech presentation viz., Free Direct Speech in his novels both frequently and effectively. One of the best examples may be drawn from *The Power and the Glory*, Part I, Chapter 2.

> 'The Governor has had a report . . . he tried to get away last week to Vera Cruz.'
>
> 'What are the Red Shirts doing that he comes to us?'
>
> 'Oh, they missed him, of course. It was just luck that he didn't catch the boat.'
>
> 'What happened to him?'
>
> 'They found his mule. The Governor says he must have him this month. Before the rains come.'
>
> 'Where was his parish?'
>
> 'Concepcion and the villages around. But he left three years ago.'
>
> 'Is anything known?'
>
> 'He can pass as a gringo. He spent six years at some American seminary. I don't know. What else, he was born in Carmen—The son of a storekeeper. Not that helps.' (22)

This long conversation between the chief and the lieutenant about the priest is developed without the reporting clause. Turn taking is made clear only by the beginning and the end of the quotation marks in each sentence. Greene seems to have used such a long passage without the reporting clause to produce certain effects. It is in this passage that for the first time the identity of the priest is revealed—that he is a priest who is hunted by the police. The anonymous whisky priest's past life is also disclosed in this conversation. The focus appears to be more on the details of the speech rather than on the speakers. Therefore the narrator's intrusion has been minimised allowing the characters to speak directly to the reader.

The second example is from *The Heart of the Matter*, Chapter 1, section 5.

> 'You have very fine car Major Scobie. You must have paid four hundred pounds for it.'
> 'One hundred and fifty,' Scobie said.
> 'I would pay you four hundred.'
> 'It isn't for sale, Yusef. Where would I get another?'
> 'Not now, but may be when you leave.'
> 'I'm not leaving.'
> 'Oh, I had heard that you were resigning, Major Scobie.'
> 'No.'
> 'We shopkeepers hear so much—but all of it is unreliable gossip.'
> 'How's business?'
> 'Oh, not bad, not good.'
> 'What I hear is that you've made several fortunes since the war. Unreliable gossip of course.' (34)

Here again, the author's choice is FDS as this passage marks the first conversation between Scobie, the protagonist and another important character, Yusef, the Syrian merchant and the smuggler who becomes the main cause of the former's ruin at the end. The relatively lengthy passage without authorial intervention allows the reader to assess the characters as well as their relationship with each other.

Another example is from *Doctor Fischer of Geneva*.

> Doctor Fischer had introduced a conflict between us, for I began to argue that after all I had nothing against Doctor Fischer . . .
>
> 'He wants you to join the Toads.'
>
> 'But I've got nothing against the Toads. Are they really as bad as you say? I've seen three of them. I admit I didn't much care for Mrs. Montgomery.'
>
> 'They weren't always Toads, I suppose. He's corrupted all of them.'
>
> 'A man can only be corrupted if he's corruptible.'
>
> 'And how do you know you aren't?'
>
> 'I don't. Perhaps it's a good thing to find out.'
>
> 'So you'll let him take you into a high place and show you all the kingdoms of the world.'
>
> I'm not Christ, and he's not Satan and I thought we'd agreed he was God Almighty although I suppose the damned God Almighty looks very like Satan.
>
> Oh, all right, she said, go and be damned. (33)

The interesting thing to be noticed here is that the NRSA switches to FDS. The author uses NRSA first to narrate the unimportant stretches of conversation between Jones and his wife and then chooses FDS. The I-narrator after reporting his speech act directly, presents Anna-Luise's response without any reporting clause. Once again here also FDS is used in the first and only argument between Jones and his wife. The argument concerns attending one of the 'abominable' parties of Doctor Fischer. His wife tries to dissuade Jones from going to the party as she sees the danger of his being corrupted by her detestable father, especially, as it happens to be the first party that Jones is to attend.

FDS is also used in the following conversation between major Scobie and Yusef when the latter is trying to trap Scobie into his trade as a first step in his blackmail.

> 'Is that a wise thing to do, Major Scobie?'
>
> 'I think it's very wise. Any kind of secret between us

two would go bad in time.'

'Just as you like, Major Scobie, but I don't want anything from you, I promise. I would like to give you things always. You will not like a refrigerator, but I thought I would perhaps take advice, information.'

'I'm listening, Yusef.'

'Tallit's a small man. He is a Christian. Father Rank and other people go to his house. They say, "if there's such a thing as an honest Syrian, then Tallit's the man." Tallit's not very successful, and that looks the same as honesty.'

'Go on.'

'Tallit's cousin is sailing in the next Portuguese boat. His luggage will be searched, of course, and nothing will be found. He will have a parrot with him in a cage. My advice, Major Scobie, is to let Tallit's cousin go and keep his parrot.'

'Why let the cousin go?'

'You do not want to show your hand to Tallit. You can easily say the parrot is suffering from a disease and must stay. He will not dare to make a fuss.'

'You mean the diamonds are in its crop?'

'Yes.'

'Has that trick been used before the Portuguese boat?'

'Yes.'

'It looks to me as if we'll have to buy an aviary.'

'Will you act on that information Major Scobie?'

'You give me information Yusef. I don't give you information.' (*The Heart of the Matter*, Part III, Ch. 1, 106)

Here also the author seems to have used FDS to focus on the informative details of the conversation.

It can be assumed from the above illustrations that Greene's use of FDS is more purposeful and meaningful. He makes it significant by employing this technique generally in crucial scenes where the speech of the main characters is presented and also in other scenes of significance. Thus the analysis of the use of FDS by Greene in his novels shows us two important things. First, FDS is employed to throw more light on the author's skill in character portrayal. Secondly, it provides better scope for the reader to understand and assess the characters and their relationship with each other depending on the situations they are placed in.

3.2.3 The Use of FIS in Presenting Speech

FIS is normally viewed as a form where the authorial voice is interposed between the reader and what the character says, so that the reader is distanced from the character's words. This can be explained if it is assumed that DS is a norm or baseline for the portrayal of speech as seen in the following figure (1981).

NRSA IS FIS DS FDS
↑
norm

The movement to the right of DS on the above scale will produce an effect of freeness as if the author has vacated the stage and left it to his characters which is seen in the illustrations of FDS. The movement to the left of the norm can be interpreted as a movement away from speech verbatim and towards the interference of the narrator. It is this distancing which allows FIS to be used as a 'vehicle for irony.' But in the case of Greene, FIS is used to produce different effects which are shown in the following examples from his novels.

> 'It was his pride. His infernal pride.'
>
> She told me how her mother loved music, which her father hated—there was no doubt at all of that hatred. Why it was she had no idea, but it was as if music taunted him with his failure to understand it, with his

> stupidity. Stupid? The man who had invented Dentophil Bouquet and founded a fortune of many million francs stupid? So her mother began to slip away to concerts on her own and at one of them she met a man who shared her love of music. They even bought discs and listened to them in secret in his flat. When Doctor Fischer talked of the caterwauling of the strings she no longer tried to argue with him—she had only to walk down a street near the butcher's, speak in a parlophone and take a lift to the third floor and listen for an hour happily to Heifetz. There was no sex between them—Anna-Luise was sure of that. (*Doctor Fischer of Geneva*, 39)

The passage starts with the speech (DS) of Anna-Luise and slips into IS, then to FIS, avoiding the continual repetition of reporting clause. The italicization of 'that' in the third sentence may indicate the contrastive stress in the speech. The use of dashes shows how the conversation is contracted. It is interesting to note the I-narrator's comment in the middle (Stupid? the man who had invented Dentophil bouquet and founded a fortune of many million francs stupid?) which increases the distance between the character's speech and the reader. The story continues for another one and a half pages in this manner, with dashes and the occasional use of contrasting modes of NRSA and DS. In this scene, the use of FIS provides immediacy and clarity to the narrative.

Another example from the same novel is:

> 'And there's my age,' I added. 'I'm old enough to be your father' thinking that perhaps I was just that, a substitute for the father she didn't love and that I owed my success to Doctor Fischer. (17)

DS and inversion are used in the first sentence which slips into IS with a reporting clause but shows some features of freeness. This may be interpreted as the I-narrator, while reporting adds his words verbatim to give the flavour of the original words spoken.

The sentence beginning with 'I added [since DS and inversion play here] . . . thinking that perhaps' exhibits subordination but offers some degree of faithfulness to the original which qualifies this passage as being in FIS. It is interesting to observe here that FIS does not involve any kind of distancing but shows some movement towards directness.

Again the third example which is from the same novel, Doctor Fischer of Geneva shows the use of different modes together in a single passage.

> 'What a feast he gave after the ceremony, my mother said. Dentophil Bouquet had already made him a fortune, you see,' she added, 'and we were neutral and the rich weren't really rationed. I suppose that might count as the first of his dinners. There was French scent for all the women and gold swizzle sticks for the men—he liked to have women at his table in those days. They didn't break up till five in the morning. (15)

Anna-Luis tells Jones about the first party of Doctor Fischer as her mother described it to her.

The passage begins with FIS where Anna-Luis is obviously reporting what her mother said. She uses the actual words verbatim and then the narration slips into DS and inversion. Again from the third sentence onwards she describes the wedding party of her parents in FIS. Here the negative syntactic features of FIS are the omission of the reporting clause and 'that' conjunction. The positive features are the retention of verb in the past tense and the third person pronouns. In this case it is one character reporting another character's version of Doctor Fischer but not the author's report of the character's speech. In other words the person whose words are reported is the same both in primary and secondary speech situations. So the retention of the third person pronoun is natural irrespective of the mode used.

One of the advantages of FIS that the novelist demonstrates is that it can easily mix with the narrative. As a result, sometimes the effects of FIS become quite unobtrusive. In the following extract from *The Heart of the Matter* the inseparability of FIS and the narrative can be observed.

> He said, 'And then in the holidays you went back to Bury?'
>
> Apparently her mother had died ten years ago, and her father was a clergy man attached in some way to the cathedral. They had a very small house on Angel Hill, perhaps she had not been as happy at Bury as at school, for she tacked back at this first opportunity to discuss the games mistress whose name was the same as her own—Helen. (BK 11, Part I, Ch. 2, 139)

After the departure of his wife, Scobie comes in contact with a child widow who tells him about her past life.

The word 'apparently' offers a clue for the reader to conclude that the author now turns to FIS. The use of past and pluperfect and the absence of the reporting clause confirm the same. Here it may be seen how smoothly FIS slips into narrative as the last sentence shows the author's inferences (from her speech) when he suddenly switches from FIS tö narrative.

In the same context from *The Heart of the Matter* another interesting case of FIS can be observed. It marks a sudden shift from FDS to FIS.

> 'Were you good at anything besides net ball?'
>
> 'I think I was next best at maths, but I was never any good at trigonometry.' In summer they went into seaport and bathed and every Saturday they had a picnic on the downs—sometime a paper-chase on ponies, and once a disastrous affair on bicycles which spread out over the whole country, and two girls didn't return till one in the morning. He listened fascinated. (138)

Scobie knows that what the girl needs in her present condition is small talk but not sympathy from others. He also realises that a girl like her cannot 'act the part of a woman' after the death of her three-week-old husband before her eyes. So he decides to listen to her childish talk which fascinates him. Here the contrast between the two modes of speech presentation puts one 'in the shadow of the other' as it appears. It allows the reader to infer the characters' attitudes towards the conversation presented.

This also shows how FIS can contrast with the other speech modes in the author's control of the 'light and shade' of conversation. The author ensures that the 'highlighting and backgrounding' is dependent on the role and attitude of the characters. Scobie's speech is highlighted and presented in DS. A part of Helen's speech is presented in DS and soon the narrator shifts to FIS and thus the reader is kept away from her speech.

The uses and effects of FIS, therefore, are many and varied as illustrated through the passages quoted above. These varied effects can be "explained naturally if FIS is viewed by virtue of its intermediary position on the scale, contrasting in different ways with alternative speech modes" (1981, 336).

WORKS CITED

Greene, Graham. *The Heart of the Matter* (London: Penguin, 1971).

Greene, Graham. *The Power and the Glory* (London: Penguin, 1940).

Greene, Graham. *Doctor Fischer of Geneva or The Bomb Party* (London: Penguin, 1980)

Leech, G.N. and Michael H. Short. *Style in Fiction: A Linguistic Introduction to English Fictional Prose*. ELS (London: Longman, 1981).

Meir, Sternberg. "How Indirect Discourse Means" in *Literary Pragmatics*, ed. Roger D. Sell (London, New York: Routledge, 1991).

Page, Norman. *Speech in the English Novel*. ELS (London: Longman, 1973).

CHAPTER 4

The Presentation of Thought

4.1 Methods of Presenting Thought in a Novel

One of the chief concerns of the novelists for the last hundred years has been how to present the flow of thought through a character's mind. Many novelists of the nineteenth and the twentieth centuries have concentrated on the portrayal of 'internal' or 'inner' speech. Thus thought presentation has been identified with the well known technique called 'stream of consciousness' or the 'interior monologue.'

Generally, it is not possible to have access to the minds of other people. But in the novel, it is imperative that the novelist enables his reader to know the feelings and attitudes of the characters. So the presentation of their thoughts like the use of soliloquy on the stage, has been considered significant. In his attempt to tell the reader what is in the minds of his characters the novelist employs various experimental techniques such as Free Indirect Thought. These attempts are "not just to report what the character thinks but also to render the character's immediate experience or consciousness of those thoughts" (1981, 337).

The methods employed by the writer in presenting the thoughts of his characters are the same as those of speech presentation and they are distinguished from one another by similar ways. The general examples given by Leech and Short are:

He wondered 'does she still love me?

(Direct Thought: DT)

Does she still love me?

(Free Direct Thought: FDT)

He wondered whether she still loved him.

(Indirect Thought: IT)

Did she still love him?

(Free Indirect Thought: FIT)

He wondered about her love for him.

(Narrative Report of Thought Act: NRTA)

These examples indicate that the modes of thought presentation, just as those of speech, can be distinguished by features from any one of the three levels of grammar, lexis and graphology. The FIT example is distinct from DT in the following features: the introductory reporting clause is removed, the first person pronoun changes to the third, the tense changes to the past and finally the interrogative form and the question mark are retained. On the other hand, the FDT version is like that of DT except for the absence of the reporting clause. The features seen in IT form are the presence of the reporting clause, subordination and a declarative form for the reported clause. In NRTA a minimal report of what is thought is given.

If the novelist allows the reader to know the thoughts of the character the reader sees everything from the character's point of view. When the novelist moves along the scale towards the free end of the thought presentation continuum, he presents the verbatim thoughts of the character with minimum intervention. This is shown in the following figure (1981).

NRTA IT FIT DT FDT

|

Norm

Before the identification of varieties of thought presentation came into existence, critics like Dujardin (N. Page 1973, 38) termed it the 'interior monologue' as stated earlier. He describes thought presentation in the novels as 'Unheard and Unspoken Speech' through which the character expresses his innermost thoughts independent of any logical organization. His contention in other words is that the interior monologue can be recognised by its purpose to reflect what he calls 'thought in a nascent state,' as well as by certain stylistic and syntactical features. Although Jane Austen and Dickens used this technique in their novels, the experimental novelists of the early twentieth century such as James Joyce, Dorothy Richardson and Virginia Woolf used it much more precisely and confidently.

Norman Page (1975, 41) has analysed an extract from *Mrs. Dalloway*, a novel by V. Woolf (1925) to show some of its distinctive features.

> Mrs. Dalloway said she would buy the flowers herself as Lucy had her work cut out for her. The doors would be taken off their hinges; Rumplemayar's men were coming, And then, thought Clarissa Dalloway, what a morning, fresh as if to children on a beach.
>
> What a lark! What a plunge! For so it had always seemed to her, when with a little squeak of the hinges, which she could hear now, she had burst open the French windows and plunged at Boulton into the open air: How fresh, how calm, stiller than this of course, the air was in the early morning: like the flap of a wave; the kiss of a wave; chill and sharp and yet (for a girl of eighteen as she then was) solemn, feeling as she did standing there at the open window, that something awful was about to happen looking at the flowers, at the trees with the smoke winding off them and the looks rising, falling, standing and cooking lentil Peter Walsh said, "Musing among the vegetable?"—was that it?—"I prefer men to cauliflowers"—was that it? He must have

said it at breakfast one morning when she had gone out on to the terrace—Peter Walsh.

Virginia Woolf moves quickly in the first two sentences of her novel from indirect speech to a freer form conveying the heroine's thoughts without the distraction of the introductory verb. This is because the narrative in the opening sentence immediately gives place to thoughts. The change of pronouns and the tense of the verbs indicate that the novelist turns to FIT. The colloquial expressions 'had her work cut out' 'what a lark!' indicate spontaneous speech rather than the formal narrative style. Here the FIT form operates at three levels—lexical, syntactical and graphological. Therefore, the style of the interior monologue is distinguishable from that of other portions of the novel.

Norman Page, in his analysis further states that such features as 'repetition,' 'self-interruption' and 'self questioning' (How fresh. . . . Was that it?) belong to spoken prose and reinforce the impression of a spontaneous flow of the thought of the character. He says that the 'looseness,' 'the casualness,' the 'absence of pattern' in the style are the result of haphazard recollections of Mrs. Dalloway. Yet, the syntax is both orderly and controlled. A great advantage that N. Page perceives in this technique is that "different elements may be combined without the formality of the usual indications of speech or thought and the often awkward transitions from one 'system' to another" (1973, 42).

On the other hand, Leech and Short (1981) view this kind of 'slipping, from narrative to FIT as a negative feature of speech and thought presentation because they feel that sometimes it is difficult to say by the use of formal linguistic criteria alone whether one is reading the thoughts of the character or the views of the narrator. Two examples are analysed in support of this point. The first one is from Dickens's *David Copperfield*.

Three years long in the aggregate, though short as they

went by. And home was very dear to me, and Agnes too—but she was not mine—she was never to be mine. She might have been, but that was past.

In this I-narration novel, where the first person pronoun can occur in FIT, the 'interpolation,' 'exclamation' and 'truncated sentences' indicate the character-narrator's emotional involvement. The reader might feel misled when he discovers that the author at last leads the story to a happy ending which he seems to deny here. But this problem can be overcome if it is interpreted as FIT.

The second example which is more problematic is from Jane Austen's *Persuasion*:

He had thought her wretchedly altered, and in the first moment of appeal, had spoken as he felt. He had not forgiven Anne Elliot. She had used him ill; deserted and disappointed him; and worse, she had shown a feebleness of character in doing so, which his own decided, confident temper could not endure.

Mary Lascellas in her book *Jane Austen and Her Art* (1965, 204) disputed the status of sentences by stating that they are either authorial or the FIS of Frederick Wentworth in conversation with his sister in chapter seven. She argues that Jane Austen's move here is an 'oversight' because it illicitly breaks the consistent portrayal of events from Anne's point of view. This argument is contradicted by Wayne C. Booth in his *Rhetoric of Fiction* (1961). He believes that what is presented here is the FIT of Wentworth but not the FIS. So in this 'momentary inside view' Wentworth's mistaken interpretation of the events of the novel is given and he does not seem to have realised this mistake till the end of the story. Wayne C. Booth further states, "It is a deliberate manipulation of inside views in order to destroy our conventional security. We are thus made to go along with Anne in her long and painful road to the discovery that Frederick loves her after all" (1961, 252). This interpretation seems preferable because of its satisfactory explanation for the shift in the viewpoint.

Thus, the author occasionally slips from narrative to interior portrayal without the reader's notice of what has occurred. When the narrator and character are merged in this way the reader tends to take the character's view. This is called 'the manipulation of point of view' by the author which can solve the problems arising due to 'slipping' discussed above. The relationship between thought and point of view is discussed in chapter six.

Thus the description of categories of thought presentation available to the novelist takes us to the study of presentation of thought in Graham Greene's fiction.

4.2 The Presentation of Thought in Graham Greene's Novels

Though the categories of thought presentation are the same as those of speech presentation, the more direct forms viz., DT and FDT produce different effects from their speech counterparts. This difference is because of the fact that the presence of an omniscient narrator is necessary in any portrayal of character thought. On the other hand, in the presentation of DS or FDS the characters talk to the reader directly with minimum authorial intervention In DT and FDT also authorial intervention appears minimal but when the character is talking to himself he is in control of his thoughts. In other words, the character's thoughts acquire a conscious quality. This is shown in *The Heart of the Matter* in the scene in which Scobie on his way home thinks about his distressed wife. He is trying to gain courage to meet his wife's 'habitual misery.'

> He forgot Fraser: he forgot everything but the scene ahead: I shall go in and say, 'Good evening, sweet heart, and she'll say, 'Good evening, darling. What kind of a day? and I'll talk and talk, but all the time I shall know

> I'm coming nearer to the moment when I shall say, 'What about you, darling,' and let the misery in. (Ch. 2, p. 56)

Here, Greene makes his protagonist consider with 'apparent verbal articulation' the conversation he is to have with his wife. Though the passage is presented in FDS without reporting clause and with less authorial intervention the presence of the omniscient narrator who keeps the character conscious of his thoughts is felt.

Sometimes, the character loses control over his thoughts because of the emotional burden. This point is clear in the extract from *The Power and the Glory*, Part three, Chapter one, where the priest is optimistic about his escape but the thought of leaving his daughter to her fate makes him feel miserable.

> In three days, he told himself, I shall be in Las Casas: I shall have confessed and been absolved, and the thought of the child on the rubbish-heap came automatically back to him with painful love. What was the good of confession when you loved the result of your crime? (176)

Here, the combination of FDT and inversion is an indication that the priest is in control of his thoughts. He is planning for a successful escape, confession and absolution at Las Casas. But immediately after these deliberations he becomes emotional with the thought of his child on the rubbish heap and his love for her. Thus he loses control over his thoughts.

It is relatively easy to distinguish FDT from other modes of presentation because the narrator's interference appears less in FDT. Another example in evidence of this, is found in the same novel. It is located in the scene where the priest, lying down in Maria's hut contemplates his predicament.

> He thought: If I go I shall meet other priests: I shall go

> to confession: I shall feel contrition and be forgiven: eternal life will begin for me all over again. The Church taught that it was every man's first duty to save his own soul. The simple ideas of hell and heaven moved in his brain. (Part two, Ch.1, p. 65)

Except the last sentence which is presented in NRTA the whole passage is in FDT giving the impression of the invisible presence of the narrator. Here, it can be observed how easily FDT can be separated from the other mode. The author, after presenting the thoughts of the priest in FDT suddenly slips into NRTA which is a minimal report of the thoughts of the priest about hell and heaven.

It is also possible for the author to combine various modes of presentation in a single passage. Greene is particularly fond of mixing various modes in his narrative. For example, the following passage from *The Heart of the Matter*, Book one, Chapter one is examined.

> 'Your wife won't like it.'
>
> 'I've been here too long to go.' He thought to himself, poor Louise, if I had left it to her, where should we be now? and he admitted straightaway that they wouldn't be here—somewhere far better, better climate, better pay, better position. She would have taken every opening for improvement. She would have steered agilely up the ladder and left the snakes alone. I've landed her here he thought, with odd premonitory sense of guilt he always felt as though he were responsible for something in the future he couldn't even foresee. He said aloud, 'You know I like the place.'
>
> 'I believe you do. I wonder why.' (17)

In his conversation with the commissioner, Scobie's momentary shift to inner speech is presented here. In fact, whether the passage commences with speech or thought is debatable. Though the quotation marks and the full stop give it the status of speech, the last sentence in the passage (he said aloud, 'you know I like the place') perhaps is the clue that the author may be presenting the character's thoughts as it logically carries the conversation further. Moreover, 'turn taking' is shown in the commissioner's response at the end of the passage: 'I believe you do. I wonder why.' Hence, the first sentence may be interpreted as the DT of Scobie who is perhaps talking to himself.

The first sentence is an example of FDT and inversion. The third sentence 'he admitted . . .' on the other hand, is in NRTA. Further, it switches to FIT and back again to DT and finally it slips into IT. The switches from one mode to another are made apparent by the use of first person pronouns (DT, FDT) and the change in tense and pronoun (FIT). Such use of various modes of thought indicates the emotional burden that the character feels which is shown lexically by the emphatic repetition of the comparative adjective 'far better, better climate, better pay, better position.' The reporting clause towards the end of the passage serves as a reminder, strengthening the reader's awareness that he is being offered Scobie's thoughts and not the narrative.

Here is another example from the same novel of the mixing of various modes of presentation.

> Leaning back against the dressing table, he tried to pray. The Lord's prayer lay as dead on his tongue as a legal document: it wasn't his daily bread that he wanted but so much more. He wanted happiness for others and solitude and peace for himself. 'I don't want to plan any more,' he said suddenly aloud. 'They wouldn't need me if I were dead. No one needs the dead. The dead can be forgotten. O God, give me death before I give them unhappiness.' But the words sounded melodramatically in his own ears. He told himself that he mustn't get hysterical: there was far too much planning to do for an hysterical man, and going downstairs again he thought three aspirins or perhaps four were what he required in

this situation—banal situation. (189)

The narrative after two sentences slips into FIT and then with a sudden strength of realisation the character voices his thoughts which continue in the free direct form (FDT) till the presentation switches to IT and then back to FIT. Here again it is significant that the use of FDT mirrors the abrupt change in emotional key which is lexically indicated, 'I don't want to plan any more.'

Just like the direct forms, the free indirect form also has a distinctive role in thought presentation. In free indirect speech (FIS) the narrator's intervention keeps the reader at a distance from the character's actual speech. But in free indirect thought (FIT) on the other hand, the opposite effect is produced in the sense that FIT takes the reader inside the character's mind. As a result, the reader gets the thoughts of the character more vividly and immediately. The reason for the distinction is that the norm or baseline for the presentation of thought is IT whereas the norm for speech presentation is DS which is illustrated below:

				norm	
Speech presentation:	NRSA	IS	FIS	DS	FDS
Thought presentation:	NRTA	IT	FIT	DT	FDT
		↑ norm			

According to Leech and Short (1981), the reason that IT mode is treated as the norm can be explained in the light of the 'semantics of reporting.' In speech as noted earlier, direct speech (DS) claims to report the actual words of the character verbatim but in IS on the other hand, the reader gets only the substance of what the character said. In thought presentation, it is not possible to present the mind of the character directly since other people's thoughts are not accessible to such direct perception which is possible in speech. In other words, thoughts in general are not verbally formulated and hence, cannot be reported verbatim.

Thus, the norms for speech and thought presentation are at different points on the continuum determining different values for FIT and FIS. FIS moves left from the norm (as shown in the figure above) and is, therefore, interpreted as a movement towards authorial intervention whereas FIT is seen as a movement towards the right, into the mind of the character keeping the reader away from the author's control. Since the direct perception of someone else's thoughts is not possible, DT is considered as a "more artificial" form. Hence, when DT is used the writer implies, 'this is what the character would have said if he had made his thoughts explicit.' Perhaps it is this explicitness which provides a conscious quality for DT and FDT which is already discussed.

This analysis explains that FIT is considered as a natural mode of presentation and therefore becomes a common device in the twentieth century novel. In the light of this analysis Greene's use of FIT is examined.

Greene seems to be fond of shifting the narrative focus to the minds of the characters. In his novels, the narrative appears to slip into FIT very often as it easily mixes with the narrative report. The following passage from *The Power and the Glory* is considered as an example.

> He began to walk across the little silent clearing towards the hut: Would they shoot him before he got to the entrance: It was like walking a plank blindfold: you didn't know at what point you would step off into space for ever. He hiccuped once and knotted his hands behind his back to stop them trembling. He had been glad in a way to turn from Miss Lehr's gate—he had never really believed that he would ever get back to Parish work and the daily Mass and the careful appearances of piety, but all the same you needed to be a little drunk to die. (186)

This is from one of the crucial scenes of the novel where the priest is trapped by the mestizo. The priest is led to the village on the pretext of hearing the death-bed confession of the Yankee who has been lying in one of the huts.

The first sentence is the narrative report. The following sentence which is a question is in FIT because it begins without the introductory reporting clause. Again the fifth one is the narrative report which slips into FIT. Here, though the narrative inseparably mixes with the character's thoughts, it is the unreported question and the personal pronoun 'you' (indicating that the priest is talking to himself) that take the reader directly to the mind of the priest.

There is another interesting example from the same novel where Greene presents the chain of thoughts in the mind of the priest when he watches Maria, the mother of his child, who gives him shelter and protection from the police.

> He watched her covertly: was this all there was in marriage, this evasion and suspicion and lack of ease? when people confessed to him in terms of passion, was this all they meant—the hard bed and the busy woman and the not talking about the past? (Part two, Ch. 1, p. 64)

The passage is full of interrogative forms. At first glance it appears to be in FDT but the third person pronoun in the third sentence gives the reader the clue that the author is reporting the thoughts of the character. Here it can be observed that, beginning with a narrative report the passage smoothly slips into FIT indicating 'freeness' from the author's narrative control.

Here is another example of FIT from *The Heart of the Matter*, Part two, Chapter three.

> He thought: I have come to the end. What years had passed since he walked up through the rain to the Nissen hut, while the sirens wailed: the moment of happiness. It was time to die after so many years. (Part two, Chapter 3, 260-61)

This short passage starts with direct thought (DT) of Scobie who thinks that he is nearing his end. His distressed and fatigued mind reveals that many years passed since he had felt any moments of happiness and it is time for him to die.

The assumption here is that the author first presents Scobie's thoughts in DT as he intends to indicate to the reader that he is now presenting the thoughts of the character but not his own interpretation. Otherwise, it is difficult in FIT to differentiate between the thoughts of the character and the narrator's words. It appears that Greene in his novels seems to avoid this ambiguity.

Similarly, in Greene's presentation what appears to be a true report (i.e., IT) soon assumes a freer form as is seen in this extract from the novel *Doctor Fischer of Geneva.*

> I thought I had tried to do just that, but I had failed, and was it for love I had tried or was it from the fear of an irremediable loneliness? (107)

Jones' reaction to Fischer's belief that people do not die for love 'except in novels' is presented through his thoughts. It seems that the I-narrator in his attempt to report the thoughts of Jones slips into FIT as if he is exploring the character's mind to reveal his real intentions to the reader.

Very often Greene uses the technique of 'slipping' from narrative to FIT or from DT to FIT to avoid ambiguity. But in the following extract from *The Power and the Glory* he directly goes into the mind of the character without any narrative report or introductory reporting clause at the beginning of the passage.

> If he left them they would be safe, and they would be free from his example. He was the only priest the children could remember: it was from him they would take their ideas of the faith. But it was from him too they took God—in their mouths. When he was gone it would be as if God in all this space between the sea and the

> mountains ceased to exist, wasn't it his duty to stay, even if they despised him, even if they were murdered for his sake? even if they were corrupted by his example? (Part two, Ch. 1, 65)

This passage sums up the priest's dilemma of whether to live with the people or to leave them to their fate like the other priests. The 'enormity' of the problem shatters him as the author says.

In the entire paragraph the priest's thoughts are presented in the Free Indirect Form without even the distraction of the introductory verb of thinking. It looks as though the author is reading the character's thoughts.

Thus, Greene shows tremendous skill and versatility in employing different modes of thought presentation both individually and in combination with other modes, in order to produce a variety of effects in his novels.

WORKS CITED

Booth, Wayne C. *The Rhetoric of Fiction* (Chicago: University of Chicago Press, 1961).

Greene, Graham. *The Heart of the Matter* (London: Penguin, 1971).

Greene, Graham. *The Power and the Glory* (London: Penguin, 1940).

Greene, Graham. *Doctor Fischer of Geneva or the Bomb Party* (London: Penguin, 1980).

Lascellas, Mary. *Jane Austen and Her Art* (London: OUP, 1965).

Leech, G.N. and M.H. Short. *Style in Fiction: A Linguistic Introduction to English Fictional Prose*. ELS (London: Longman, 1981).

Page, Norman. *Speech in the English Novel*. ELS (London: Longman, 1973).

Woolf, Virginia. *Mrs. Dalloway* (London: Hogarth, 1925).

CHAPTER 5

Speech and Thought Presentation: Pedagogic Implications

In the preceding chapters I have concentrated on the problem of how the author represents speech in a medium which is not speech and what means he uses in presenting speech in his novels. I have also discussed how the variety of speech forms are exploited by the author to create particular effects. In this chapter, my attempt is two fold: first, to demonstrate how the author's use of the variety of speech presentations contributes to the total communicative effect of the novel; secondly, to discuss the implications that this kind of analysis leaves for the teachers as well as the students of literature. In other words, we are trying to address ourselves to the question: what is the purpose that motivates the author in selecting a particular way to represent the thoughts or speech of the character at any given point in the novel.

In a novel, the choice of a particular form of speech or thought presentation is determined by two purposes—(1) The Communicative purpose (2) The Stylistic purpose. The Communicative purpose refers to the information that the author is trying to convey through his choice of linguistic features within the context of the utterance. The Stylistic purpose is concerned with the choice of a particular form of speech presentation in relation to the other utterances in the discourse of the novel (Tom Hutchinson, 1988: Ch. 5).

5.1 Communicative Purpose

While analysing the speech presentation techniques we have learnt that, in the novel, the author tries to establish a triangular relationship between himself and the reader and the characters. The speech presentation techniques are the strategies or the means with which he maintains this relationship. We came to know that FDS is the freer version of DS where the author's intervention is minimised leaving the characters to speak on their own (to the reader). Similarly FIS, the freer version of IS, is not a mere report but involves the 'flavour of character speech' to some extent. Hence, the mechanical conversion of DS into IS or vice versa is not appropriate in the context of the novel. The author must make a careful choice of the various modes of representation of speech and thought in the whole attempt of communicating his ideas to the readers. Therefore, speech and thought presentation techniques are not just the intuitive choices of the author, but they are largely dependent on the careful and deliberate selection of the writer whose prime purpose is to present his theme as effectively as possible.

The speech presentation techniques in the novel are variants of speech fulfilling different functions. DS is the presentation of actual words of the character verbatim. IS is the mere report of the character's speech for the benefit of the reader who is denied access to the actual interaction. But what about FDS and FIS? The explanation is like this: grammatically DS and IS are characterised by the different reference systems such as reference of time, place, persons, etc. [cf. ch. 2]. But in the context of the novel, this distinction is inadequate when DS exclusively operates within the world of characters and IS operates between two worlds—the world of the reporter and the reported. In IS, the reader is distanced from the world of the characters. How far he is distanced from that world is a variable which the author alone can manipulate to suit his purposes. This variant is called FIS which can be drawn on the reference system of the two worlds to produce a variety of permutations. Similarly, how close is the reader to character's speech is dependent upon the use of another variant called FDS which is also manipulated by the author. The author acts as a mediator between the reader and the character. In FDS as we have noted earlier (cf. ch. 2) the author vacates the stage as it were and allows his characters directly speak to the reader. So, with these four meaningful categories of speech presentation the author establishes the triangular relationship between himself and the characters and the reader. In our interpretation we have added the NRSA category which is more indirect than the IS and thus acts as a bridge between the speech presentation and narrative. Of all these five categories, only the DS form can be considered as the most discrete, direct and easily identifiable type of presentation. These varieties, as shown earlier in this book form a line ranging from NRSA to FDS with each type merging into the next [cf. ch. 3]. This important distinction of speech presentation techniques, involving many features such as time and place references, personal relationships, emotive expressions enables the author to conjure up several permutations and thus enhances the total communicative effect of the novel.

5.2 The Stylistic Purpose

I have analysed in this book how Greene achieves tremendous effects by employing various permutations of speech presentation techniques. In this chapter, the focus is on the question of why any particular variety of speech presentation is preferred to the other in any given situation. This explains the stylistic purpose of the author in detail.

Graham Greene uses the permutation of FDS/FIS/DS/IS and NRSA to achieve certain specific effects in telling the story. The writer's stylistic purpose is divided into five categories for pedagogic purposes. They are as follows:

5.2.1 Summarising

In the novel whenever the author intends to summarise the character's speech he turns to IS/IT. The ability to summarise is visualised as one of the greatest advantages of reported speech. Greene's technique in summarising character's speech is interesting. He often turns to FIS or NRSA whenever he summarizes. For instance, look at the following extract from the novel, *Doctor Fischer of Geneva*.

> He told her he forgave her which only increased her sense of guilt, for surely there had to be something to forgive, but he told her also that he could never forget her betrayal—what betrayal? So he would wake her in the night to stab her with his goad again. She learnt that he had discovered the name of her friend—that harmless little lover of music—and he went to the man's employer and gave him fifty thousand francs to sack him without a reference. 'That was Mr. Kips,' she said. Her friend was only a clerk,—he wasn't important—he was no better than a clone that you could replace with another clone. His only distinguishing feature had been his love of music and Mr. Kips knew nothing of that. To Doctor Fischer it was an added humiliation that the man earned so little. He wouldn't have minded being betrayed by another millionaire—or so her mother believed.

This paragraph beautifully summarizes the long and intermittent conversations between Anna-Luise and the I-narrator Jones. The tense and pronoun system used by the author indicate that what Anna-Luise says is not given verbatim. But yet the reader is not totally distanced from what is stated as in true IS. The reporting clause is almost omitted and the reader feels that he is listening to the I-narrator. Interestingly, we find certain elements such as exclamations/interrogative forms (e.g. what betrayal?) in the narrative which are generally altered in what is called true IS.

Here, the use of FIS enables Greene to summarise the long and perhaps many conversations that the I-narrator had with his wife about the misery of her mother's life without losing the effect of actual conversation. As it is noticed in the conversation, this effect is heightened by the use of DS in the middle of the report.

5.2.2 Contrasting

Another striking effect that the speech presentation forms produce is to provide contrasts between the speakers. In the following extract, Greene's use of FDS-DS-narrative marks a memorable contrast among the three characters—Jones, the I-narrator, his wife, Anna-Luise and Doctor Fischer. [As we have noticed earlier, Greene uses FDS-DS-narrative combination whenever he highlights or brings out a sharp contrast between the characters.]

> The first he knew about it was at the first of my father's special dinners. Everyone had a small and magnificent present—something in gold or platinum—beside his plate, except Mr. Kips who had a big brown paper parcel containing a specially bound copy of the book in red morocco. He must have been furious, but he had to pretend to be amused before the other guests, "But why poor Mr. Kips? I asked— . . . . "Uh I'll have fun with all of them in time," he told me. "Then you'll lose all your friends in time . . ." he said "all my friends are rich and the rich are the greediest. The rich have no pride except in their possessions. You only have to be careful with the poor."
>
> 'Then we are safe.' I said. 'We aren't rich' 'yes but perhaps we aren't poor enough for him.' She had a wisdom which I couldn't match perhaps that was another of the reasons why I loved her. (*Doctor Fischer of Geneva*)

In this sequence Greene sets up a pattern of FIS for the long conversation between Jones and his wife when the latter describes her father's peculiar parties. But the final exchange breaks into DS to highlight the contrast which is completed by the narrative.

5.2.3 Distancing

Distancing, another category of the author's stylistic purposes, is often employed whenever the author intends to keep the reader distanced from what is said by the character but yet provide some 'flavour of the character's speech.' For instance, look at this example from *The Heart of the Matter*.

> He listened with the intense interest one feels in a stranger's life, the interest the young mistake for love. He felt the security of his age sitting there listening with a glass of gin in his hand and the rain coming down. She told him her school was on the downs just behind seaport: they had a French mistress called Mlle Depont who had a vile temper. The head mistress could read Greek just like English—Virgil . . .
>
> 'I always thought Virgil was Latin.'
>
> 'Oh yes. I meant Homer. I wasn't any good at classics.'
>
> 'Were you good at anything besides net ball?'
>
> In summer they went into sea port and bathed and every Saturday they had a picnic on the downs.

In this interchange between Scobie and the women, Greene achieves the effect of distance when he uses IS and FIS for the speech of the woman. Here the use of indirect forms create an air of uncertainty. But yet the sudden change to DS perhaps provides the reader with a flavour of the woman's speech. Here the major part of the woman's speech is set in FIS and not in IS, only to produce on the reader the effect of seeing her with 'intense interest' one feels in a stranger's life.

5.2.4 Presenting the Character's Viewpoint

Besides the 'local' effects that are discussed so far, speech presentation types also play a major role in determining the overall strategy of the author with which he manipulates the reader's view of the characters.

The analysis of Greene's novels especially *The Heart of the Matter* and *Doctor Fischer of Geneva* shows us that from the beginning the story is seen from the protagonists' viewpoint. There are several passages in the text (some of them are analysed in this book) representing the main character's thoughts. But the reader is seldom given a chance to peep into the minds of the women (Louise, Helen and Anna-Luis). He is often kept at a distance from what these women say or think more than from what Scobie or Jones think about them. Although they are referred by their names they are made less intimate to the reader. Greene creates these effects by his selective use of direct and indirect forms which is of course very complex as is seen throughout. Sometimes the complexity arises when the main character's speech is blended into the narrative. This takes us to another important category of the author's stylistic purpose, Blending.

5.2.5 Blending

Greene often blends the character's speech into the narrative for various purposes which are discussed earlier. Sometimes his purpose of doing this appears to be establishing the character's viewpoint. For instance, look at the following extract from the same context of the same novel, *The Heart of the Matter*.

> He did know, for he had read the report. He knew exactly the water ration for each person in the boat—a cupful twice a day, which had been reduced after twenty one days to half a cupful. That had been maintained until within twenty-four hours of the rescue mainly be-

> cause the deaths had left a small surplus. Behind the school buildings of seaport, the totempole of the net ball game, he was aware of the intolerable surge, lifting the boat and dropping it again, . . . 'I was miserable when I left—it was the end of July. I cried in the taxi all the way to the station.' Scobie counted the months—July to April: nine months. (*The Heart of the Matter*)

The sudden shift from narrative to speech in the passage makes it difficult for the reader to decide whether the author is representing the thoughts of the character or it is an FIS representation of what Scobie said to the girl. Greene seems to be making the distinction deliberately ambiguous. As a result, Scobie's thoughts are merged into the narrative and with the effect of blending the reader is able to see the story from the character's eyes. Contrastingly, the girl's thoughts are never represented. On several occasions in the novel, FIS is used mainly to report what Scobie had heard from the girl and thus distancing her from the reader. On the contrary, the girl's speech is always presented in DS, perhaps to show the contrast between the speakers.

Thus by the application of important strategies such as blending, contrasting, distancing, Greene is able to achieve strikingly different effects with speech presentation techniques. These specific categories of the author's stylistic purpose are of immense pedagogic value as they serve as a major contribution to Graham Greene's art of telling the tale.

In fact, these categories play a significant role in cinematography. The media analysts consider them as important criteria for evaluating and appreciating a film. But in fiction they tend to be overlooked by the literary critics because the aim of literature seems to be largely dependent on the story. On the contrary, the basic aspect of narratology is the grammar of narrative and the analysis of it explains and justifies the intuitive responses of the reader. Moreover, the prime objective of the literature programme is to create and promote informed readership. Hence by exploring and explaining Graham Greene's narrative this book aims to provide some important tools for the student of literature to analyse and appreciate any literary and non-literary narration and thus fulfilling the objectives of pedagogy.

WORKS CITED

Greene, Graham. *The Heart of the Matter* (England: Penguin, 1971).

Greene, Graham. *Doctor Fischer of Geneva or The Bomb Party* (England: Penguin, 1980).

Short, Mike, ed., *Reading, Analysing and Teaching Literature* (London: Longman, 1988).

CHAPTER 6

Point of View

In narrative writing such as the novel, there is a distinction between the story and the point of view from which the story is narrated. Some novels are narrated from the point of view of an omniscient narrator who has privileged access to the thoughts and feelings of characters which an external observer lacks. He can also foresee the events of the future. In some, the novelist knows little about the character's feelings. In another type of narration the events of the narrative are viewed from the perspective of one or more characters with great emphasis on the character's private responses to people and events. For example, Virginia Woolf's novels are representative of this mode of narration.

Roger Fowler (1986, 127) analyses some of the striking variations in point of view. According to Fowler, there are three types of point of view: spatio-temporal point of view, psychological point of view and ideological point of view.

6.1 Spatio-Temporal Point of View

In temporal point of view, the reader gets an impression of events moving rapidly or slowly in a continuous chain or isolated segments. Temporal point of view also refer to 'disruptions of the natural flow of time' by flashbacks, previsions or the interweaving of the stories related to different time spheres. Just as in painting where the viewer sees some objects near, some far, some focused and some less clear, in the novel also, the reader is led by the organisation of its language and imagines the objects, people, buildings and landscapes as existing in a certain spatial relationship to one another.

One of the best examples of spatio-temporal point of view is found in *The Power and the Glory.* In the opening scene of the novel, the author presents a picturesque description of the objects, places and people etc.

> Mr. Tench went out to look for his ether cylinder, into the blazing Mexican sun and the bleaching dust. A few vultures looked down from the roof with shabby indifference: he wasn't carrion yet. A faint feeling of rebellion stirred in Mr. Tench's heart and he wrenched up a piece of the road with splintering finger nails and tossed it feebly towards them. One rose and flapped across the tower: over the tiny plaza, over the bust of an ex-president, ex-general, ex-human being, over the two stalls which sold mineral water, towards the river and the sea. It wouldn't find anything there: the sharks looked after the carrion on that side. Mr. Tench went on across the plaza. (7-8)

The description of the port scene which continues for two pages brings before the reader's eyes vivid visuals of the 'blazing sun' 'bleaching dust' and the two vultures sitting on the roof. The dryness of life is indicated through the use of strong objectives in the first half of the passage (blazing, bleaching, shabby and faint). The second half describes the spatial content of the prose. The prepositions like 'towards,' 'across,' 'over' and 'on' not only refer to locations but also relate them relevantly. The language is organised in a sequence and takes the reader along with the vulture from place to place in a definite order. Here, the reader's eye comes back again and stops at the plaza where Mr. Tench goes and meets a man with a gun sitting in a small patch against a wall. From there the reader's eye moves along with Mr.

Tench past the Treasury, towards the quay. The entire one and a half pages description is worth studying for the organisation of these visual movements and transitions. The linguistic choices of the author in the passage control the reader's perception towards the shift of focus and the relationship among the objects. Thus, the language guides the reader to perceive carefully, slowly and relevantly.

6.2 Ideological Point of View

Ideological point of view in a narrative text refers to the set of values of belief systems communicated through the text. The novel gives an interpretation of the world it represents. For example, Tolstoy's Christianity, Lawrence's Celebration of Sexuality, Greene's Catholicism etc. represent the content of the ideology which is to be identified in the novel.

The important questions that arise in considering the point of view on the ideological plane are: (1) who conveys the ideology? (2) is it the author speaking through the narrative voice, or is it a character or characters? (3) Is there a single dominating world view, or a plurality of ideological positions?

In ideological point of view, a narrator or a character may directly indicate his or her judgements and beliefs by the use of a variety of modal structures. "Modality is the means by which people express their degree of commitment to the truth of the propositions they utter and their view on the desirability or otherwise of the states of affairs referred to." (Fowler 1986, 131).

A checklist of various model expressions in language is presented here.

Modal Auxiliaries: Some important modal auxiliaries are may, might, must, will, shall, should, could, needs to and ought to. These words signal caution and confidence to various degrees. The strongly positive modals such as 'must' have the additional meaning of necessity or obligation.

Modal Adverbs or Sentence Adverbs: Certainly, surely, probably, perhaps etc. are some of the modal adverbs.
Evaluative Adjectives and Adverbs: Fortunately, luckily, regrettably and many other words like these come under this category.
Verbs of Knowledge, Prediction, Evaluation: Seem, believe, guess, foresee, approve, dislike are some of the words which belong to this category.
Generic Sentences: These are generalised propositions claiming universal truth and are generally placed in syntax which is used in proverbs and scientific laws.

These are some of the modal expressions which are found in many novels, listed by Roger Fowler (1986, 131-32).

The Power and the Glory offers a good example of plural ideological structure. Plural ideology is interesting because it deals with different value systems which are in a conflicting relationship with each other. In this novel, the whisky priest's Catholicism and the lieutenant's totalitarianism are in conflict with each other. Outwardly, the hunter is a better man than the hunted. While the hunter has force and character, the hunted is reduced to 'drunken giggling insignificance.' This confrontation of seeming unequals gives the novel its final force. Though the lieutenant's victory is apparent, the real victory is God's. Even as the whisky priest dies and finds salvation, another priest arrives to carry on the mission at the risk of his life.

The confrontation develops throughout the book. The two ideologies clash when the priest and the lieutenant confront each other in the last scene where the priest is caught by the lieutenant. The following is the manifestation of the priest's point of view.

> 'Perhaps it is I've never got your ideas straight. We've always said the poor are blessed and the rich are going to find it hard to get into heaven. Why should we make it hard for the poor man too? Oh, I know we are told to

> give to the poor, to see they are not hungry—hunger can make a man do evil just as much as money can. But why should we give the poor power? It's better to let him die in dirt and wake in heaven—so long as we don't push his face in the dirt.' . . .
>
> Oh, the priest said, 'that's another thing altogether—God is love. I don't say the heart doesn't feel a taste of it, but what a taste. The smallest glass of love mixed with a pint pot of ditch-water. We wouldn't recognise that love. It might even look like hate. It would be enough to scare us—god's love. It set fire a bush in the desert, didn't it, and smashed open graves and set the dead walking in the dark. Oh, a man like me would run a mile to get away if he felt that love around.' (Part three, Ch. 3, 199)

The entire conversation of nine to twelve pages puts forth before the reader the ideologies of the two key persons of the novel—the hunted and the hunter. The use of modal auxiliary verbs such as should, can, would and might indicate caution, faith and confidence in the priest's speech.

Contrarily, the lieutenant expresses his viewpoint—the totalitarian view.

> 'It's your ideas.' The lieutenant sweated a little in the hot steamy air. He said, you are so cunning, you people. But tell me this—what have you ever done in Mexico for us? Have you ever told a landlord he shouldn't beat his peon—Oh, yes, I know, in the confessional perhaps, and it's your duty, isn't it, to forget it at once. You come out and have dinner with him and it's your duty not to know that he has murdered a peasant. That's all finished. He's left it behind in your box. . . .
>
> 'Well we have ideas too.' The lieutenant was saying, 'No more money for saying prayers, no more money for building places to say prayers in. We'll give people food

> instead, teach them to read, give them books. We'll see they don't suffer. (Part three, Ch. 3, 194)

The use of personal pronouns 'you' and 'we' shows the contrast in ideologies and the entire language signals contempt of various degrees.

Another direct way of presenting the ideological point of view is found in *Doctor Fischer of Geneva* or *The Bomb Party*. In one of his parties, Doctor Fischer projects his ideology through a variety of modal expressions.

> 'Is God greedy?'
>
> 'Oh, don't think for a moment. I believe in him any more than I believe in the devil, but I have always found theology an amusing intellectual game. Albert, Mrs. Montgomery has finished her porridge. You can take her plate. What was I saying?'
>
> 'That god is greedy.'
>
> 'Well, the believers and the sentimentalists say that he is greedy for our love. I prefer to think that, judging from the world he is supposed to have made, he can only be greedy for our humiliation, and that greed how could he ever exhaust? It's bottomless. The world grows more and more miserable while he twists the endless screw, though he gives us presents—for a universal suicide would defeat his purpose—to alleviate the humiliations we suffer. A cancer of the rectum, a streaming cold, incontinence. For example, you are a poor man, so he gives you a small present, my daughter, to keep you satisfied a little longer.
>
> 'Don't I wish to humiliate? and they say he made us in his image. Perhaps he found he was a rather bad craftsman and he is disappointed in the result.' (61-62)

The evaluative modalizers in Doctor Fischer's speech such as 'greedy,' 'miserable,' bottomless' and double adjective phrases like 'amusing intellectual' indicate a kind of measured syntax that reflects the doctor's viewpoint rather strongly. Modality is prominent not only in evaluative adjectives, but in generic sentences also such as: 'the believers and the sentimentalists say,' 'the world grows more and more miserable' etc. Doctor Fischer's ideology becomes explicit (with the announcements of his beliefs) though these modal devices which indicate his personality and also his attitude towards the rich. He laughs and makes fun of the greed in the rich. He mocks them, insults them but gives them expensive presents which he says is a kind of alleviation for the humiliation they suffer at his hands. He believes that their greed certainly isn't limited by pride. Ironically he, being rich, exhibits enormous pride consciously or unconsciously. The use of verbs of knowledge and evaluation in his pompous speech like 'believe,' 'prefer,' 'judge' reflects his pride in its intensity. In other words, the doctor's language is full of verba sentiendi; a term used by Upensky quoted by R. Fowler (1986, 136) to mean the words denoting feelings, thoughts and perceptions which are primary signals of a subjective point of view.

6.3 Psychological Point of View

The third category of point of view is 'psychological' or 'perceptual' point of view. This field is further divided into two categories with subtypes. The basic distinction is between the internal and external perspective. However, we are concerned with 'internal' narration as Greene's fiction provides good examples of this type of narration.

Type A of 'internal' narration is a narration from the point of view within a character's consciousness expressing his or her feelings about the events and characters of the story. Type B is a narration from the point of view of the 'omniscient author' who has accessibility to the thoughts and feelings of the characters.

In type A, the first person narration is distinguished by the prominent use of first person singular pronouns and the use of the present tense referring to the present time of the act of narration. The presence of the participating narrator is "highlighted by foregrounded modality stressing his judgements and opinions." (1986)

Greene is particularly fond of exploring the internal processes of his characters. The following extract from *Doctor Fischer of Geneva* exemplifies the I-narrator's thought process.

> But how does one convey happiness? Unhappiness we can so easily describe—I was unhappy we say, because . . . We remember this and that, giving good reasons, but happiness is like one of those 'islands far out in the Pacific which has been reported by sailors when it emerges from the haze where no cartographer has ever marked it. The island disappears again for a generation but no navigator is quite certain that it only existed in the imagination of some long dead lookout. I tell myself over and over again how happy I was in those weeks but when I search my head for the reason I can find nothing adequate to explain my happiness. (44)

In this passage, the reader is invited to see or understand the perceptions of the character-narrator. The I pronoun occurs quite frequently. The evaluative modal adjectives are 'good' (reasons), 'quite certain,' 'adequate,' 'long dead' which indicate the speaker's world view. The generic expressions are 'happiness is like one of those islands, 'reported by sailors,' 'existed in the imagination,' etc. Jones applies his knowledge of the world to his own experience and thus is trying to judge his own happiness. It can be observed that the language shows the character's subjective point of view enriched with 'verba sentiendi' (words denoting feelings, thoughts and perceptions). He often refers to his inner processes: 'I tell myself over and over again,' 'I reach my head for the reason.' The expressions denote reflection and judgement.

Type B of 'internal' narration is an omniscient narrator's report of the character's motives and feelings. The major difference between type A and type B is that in type B the modal expressions may not indicate the character's world view but they are framed by authorial ideology.

In a passage from *The Heart of the Matter*, this kind of point of view is exemplified.

> Scobie thought that a man was surely entitled to that much revenge. Revenge was good for the character: out of revenge grew forgiveness. He began to whistle driving back to Kru town. He was almost happy: he only needed to be quite certain that nothing had happened at the club after he left, that at this moment, 10.55 P.M., Louise was at ease, content. He could face the next hour when the next train arrived. (Part one, Ch. 1, p. 39)

Here the author gives an account of the mental process of Scobie, his feelings and perceptions. The choice of diction denotes intentions, emotions and thoughts of the character. But unlike the earlier example, here the lexical choices or the syntactic patterns may not indicate Scobie's world view. Instead, they represent the author's ideology. Therefore, the generic sentence, 'Revenge was good for the character: out of revenge grew forgiveness' may reveal the author's viewpoint. The point here is that these words do not fully manifest Scobie's thought process as is seen in the internal narration of type A. Thus, the mingling of type A and B marks an important stylistic device called FIT which is already discussed in chapter four.

There is an intricate relationship between the thoughts and the point of view of a character. While presenting the thoughts of that character in his novel, the author invites the reader to look at everything from his (the character's) point of view. That character becomes the 'reflector' of fiction. But sometimes the author can represent the character's point of view without presenting his thoughts. For example, in the following extract from *The Heart of the Matter*, two persons' point of view is indicated keeping their thoughts to the minimum.

> When he found her in the bed room under the mosquito-net she reminded him of a dog or a cat, she was so completely 'out.' Her hair was matted, her eyes closed. He stood very still like a spy in a foreign territory, and indeed he was in a foreign territory now. If home for him meant reduction of things to a friendly unchanging minimum, home to her was accumulation. (Part one, Ch. 1, p. 21)

Here Scobie's and his wife's feelings and attitudes to each other are presented without their thoughts being presented.

Similarly a character's point of view can be represented without presenting even his state of mind. Instead, the author portrays scenes and events as they appeared to the character concerned. In the following passage from *The Power and the Glory*, the reader can see things from the viewpoint of the dentist, Mr. Tench.

> A child stood in the doorway asking for a doctor. He wore a big hat and had stupid brown eyes. Behind him two mules stamped and whistled on the hot beaten road. Mr. Tench said he was the stranger couched in the rocking chair, gazing with an effect of prayer, entreaty. . . . The child said there was a new doctor in town: the old one had fever and wouldn't stir. His mother was sick.
>
> A vague memory stirred in Mr. Tench's brain. He said with an air of discovery, 'why, you're a doctor, aren't you?' (Part one, Ch. 1, p. 16)

Here the omniscient narrator is restricting himself to the perception of Mr. Tench who knows the priest only as a stranger and a quack. The linguistic forms employed are appropriate to the character from whose point of view the reader sees things. Though the expressions like 'gazing with an effect of prayer, entreaty' give the clues about the identity of the stranger, the reader is misled by the assertive locution made by Mr. Tench with an air of discovery that the stranger is a doctor. The omniscient author knows who the stranger is. But yet, the reader must assume that he is being invited to look at the events from the point of view of Mr. Tench.

Thus, there are many variations of point of view that the author can achieve through manipulation of the narrator's voice in relation to the voices of the characters in the novel.

WORKS CITED

Fowler, Roger. *Linguistic Criticism* (Oxford, New York: OUP, 1986).

Greene, Graham. *Doctor Fischer of Geneva or The Bomb Party* (London: Penguin, 1980).

Greene, Graham. *The Heart of the Matter* (London: Penguin, 1971).

Greene, Graham. *The Power and the Glory* (London: Penguin, 1940).

Conclusion

To a large extent, the novels of Graham Greene analysed in this book lend themselves readily, to the application of Speech and Thought presentation techniques proposed by Norman Page (1973) and Leech and Short (1981).

The conversational implicature drawn from the speech between Scobie and Yusef in *The Heart of the Matter*, and Jones and the servant of Doctor Fischer in *Doctor Fischer of Geneva* offer an important discovery. Interpersonal factors such as attitude, tension and conflict and also the participant's relation with his interlocutor make the speaker violate the 'cooperative principle.' On the other hand, the adherence to the cooperative principle is observed to be greater in the one sided conversation between the author and the reader which is revealed in the generic comments made by the author both in *The Power and the Glory* and *Doctor Fischer of Geneva*.

The conversational maxims can be applied not only to ordinary speech but also to the fictional speech. Further, the application demonstrates how the reader is able to draw implicature both from the character's speech and the author's commentary.

The speech presentation techniques employed by Graham Greene are singularly striking. The use of FDS in his novels gains significance by promoting a better understanding of his characters and their relationships unlike in the novels of Hemingway and James Joyce, where there seems to be a deliberate attempt to create a kind of ambiguity.

Similarly, the use of FIS in the novels is marked by ease

and alacrity with which it inseparably mixes with the narrative and contrasts with the other speech modes such as DS, IS and NRSA.

The thought presentation techniques employed by Greene, especially FDT and FIT also produce various effects such as economy of fiction. Furthermore, Greene's impersonality of fictional art is revealed through his unique way of mixing various modes in the narrative, enabling the reader to penetrate into the minds of the characters.

Greene's tremendous skill, both in the narration and character delineation is revealed when he presents the thoughts of a character without presenting the character's point of view and vice versa.

Thus, the use of speech and thought presentation as a means of varying point of view, tone and distance in Greene's fiction achieves great versatility. This versatility arises mainly because of the fine gradations that this device offers not only among the speech and thought categories but also between them and the author's narrative report. That is the reason why overlapping is seen among the speech and thought modes. For example, the effects of IS, IT, NRSA and NRTA are not discussed individually as these modes are found to be used in combination with the other modes.

Techniques such as FDS and FIS in Greene's novels are extremely useful in the interpretation of dialogue. For example, the 'tactical effect' produced by FIS and FIT offers a new interpretation to the dialogue which is shown in chapters three and four. These devices help in capturing the distinction between the author's voice and the voice which comes from inside the novel that may or may not be perceived by the reader.

This kind of analysis of Graham Greene's novels certainly throws a new light on the reading of the text by making explicit the stylistic strategies employed by Greene in order to achieve various effects through narrative technique.

The crucial problem in the teaching of literature as Widdowson (1975) states, is to perceive when and to what extent the teacher exerts control over the learner in the process of evaluating and appreciating a literary work. He also feels that indifference to this problem may lead the learner to either confusion or blind acceptance of ready-made critical judgements. Hence, the pragmatic approach adopted in this book is meant essentially to serve a pedagogic purpose: to develop in learners an awareness of how literature functions as a discourse and so to give them some new ways of interpretation. As has been argued in the Introduction to this book, the claim is not that stylistic analysis can replace literary criticism but that it can certainly prepare the way for it to operate more effectively.

It has been emphasized in this book that the value of stylistic analysis is perceived only when it provides the learner with necessary means whereby he can relate his own experience of language to any literary writing and thus extends and enriches that experience. As Widdowson rightly points out, the establishment of such a relationship can serve as a base for the learner to make either literary criticism or any teaching technique derived from it conduct its functions effectively. If seen in this light, the approach presented in this book becomes one of the significant steps to the way of literary appreciation.

Bibliography

Adinarayana, L. (1981). "A Reading of Greene's *It's a Battlefield.*" *Literary Endeavour*. July-Dec, 3 (1-2), 54-64.

______. (1984). "Greene's *Our Man in Havana*: A Study of its Narrative Structure." *Literary Endeavour* (1984), 4. 22-29.

Brumfit, C.J. (1983). *Teaching Literature Overseas: Language-based Approaches.* Oxford: Pergamon Press.

Carter, R.A., ed. (1982). *Language and Literature.* Allen & Unwin.

Chatman, Seymour and Samuel R. Levin, ed. (1967). *Essays on the Language of Literature*. Boston: Houghton Mifflin.

Cole, Peter, ed. (1978). *Pragmatics: Syntax and Semantics.* Vol. 9 (24 Vols.) New York: Academic Press.

______. (1981). *Radical Pragmatics.* New York: Academic Press.

Couto, Maria. (1988). *Graham Greene on the Frontier.* London: The Macmillan Press.

Crystal, David and Derek Davy. (1969). *Investigating English Style.* London: Longman. Bloomington: Indiana University Press.

Deyes, A. (1982). "Discourse Analysis and Literary Interpretation." *English Language Teaching*, 36, 119-24.

Dombrowski, Theo Q. (1989). "Graham Greene: Technique of Intensity." *Ariel*, 6, IV (1989), 29-38.

Ehrlich, Susan (1990). *Point of View: A Linguistic Analysis of Literary Style.* London & New York: Routledge.

Evans, R.O. (1963). *Greene: Some Critical Considerations.* Lexington: University of Kentugy Press.

Ferns, C.S. (1985). "'Brown is not Greene' Narrative Role in *The Comedian.*" *Coll L.*, Winter, 12 (1), 60-67.

Fish, Stanely. (1980). *Is there a text in this class? The authority of interpretative communities.* Cambridge, Mass.: Harward University Press.

Fowler, R. (1971). *The Languages of Literature: Some Linguistic Contributions to Criticism.* London: Routledge & Kegan Paul.

______, ed. (1975). "'Style and Structure in Literature." *Essays in the New Stylistics.* Ithaca, N.Y.: Cornell University Press.

______. (1981). *Literature as Social Discourse: The Practice of Linguistic Criticism.* London: Batsford.

Freeman, Donald C., ed. (1970). *Linguistics and Literary Style.* New York: Holt, Rinehart & Winston.

______. (1981). *Essays in Modern Stylistics.* London: Methuen.

Gazdar, Gerald. (1979). *Pragmatics: Implicature, Presupposition and Logical Form.* New York: Academic Press.

Greene, Graham. (1940). *The Power and the Glory.* London: Penguin.

______. (1971). *The Heart of the Matter.* London: Penguin.

______. (1980). *Doctor Fischer of Geneva or The Bomb Party.* London: Penguin.

Grob, Alan. (1969). "*The Power and the Glory*: Graham Greene's Argument from Design." *Criticism*, Vol. 11 (1969), 1-30.

Halliday, M.A.K. (1970). "Descriptive Linguistics in Literary Studies." *Linguistics and Literary Style*, ed. D.C. Freeman. New York: Holt, Reinehart & Winston, 57-72.

Harnish, Robert M. (1976). "Logical Form and Implicature." *An Integrated Theory of Linguistic Ability*, ed. Thomas G. Bever et al. New York: Crowell, 313-91.

Harris, R. (1979). "The Descriptive Interpretation of Performative Utterances," *Journal of Linguistics*, 14, 331-34.

Herbert, Haber R. (1957). "The Two Worlds of Graham Greene," *Modern Fiction Studies*, vol. 111, No. 3, Autumn, 256-68.

Hutchinson, Tom. (1988). "Speech Presentations in Fiction with reference to *The Tiger Moth* by H.E. Bates" in Mike Short, ed., 120-45.

Karttunen, Lauri and Stanley Peters. (1979). "Conversational Implicature." *Oh & Dinnen*, 1-56.

Darey, Kynel. (1984). "A Conversation with Graham Greene." *IONC*, June, 13 (3), 2-6

Leech, G.N. (1980). *Explorations in Semantics and Pragmatics.* Amsterdam: Benjaminis.

______. (1985). "Stylistics." *Discourse and Literature*, ed. T.A. Van Dijk. Amsterdam: Benjaminis, 39-57.

______. (1987). "Stylistics and Functionalism" in Fabb et al. (1987): 76-88.

Leigh, David J.S.J. (1985). "The Structure of Greene's *The Honor-*

ary Consul."Renascence, Autumn, 38 (1) (1985), 13-24.

Levinson, Stephen C. (1983). *Pragmatics.* Cambridge & New York: Cambridge University Press.

Lewis, R.W.B. (1957). "The Ideology of Graham Greene" *Modern Fiction Studies*, Vol. III, No. 3, Autumn, 195-215.

Lodge, David. (1966). *Graham Greene.* Columbia: Columbia University Press.

______. (1966). *Language of Fiction: Essays in Criticism and Verbal Analysis of the English Novel.* London: Routledge and Kegan Paul.

Mesnet, Maria-Beatrice. (1984). *Graham Greene and "The Heart of the Matter."* London: The Cresset Press.

Norman, Macleod. (1983). "'This strange rather sad story,' The Reflexive Design of Graham Greene's *The Third Man.*" *DR*, Summer, 63 (2), 217-41.

Pattern, Karl. (1957). "The Structure of *The Power and the Glory.*" *Modern Fiction Studies*, Vol. III, No. 3, Autumn, 225-34.

Pratt, M.L. (1977). *Toward a Speech Act Theory of Literary Discourse.* Bloomington: Indiana University Press.

Rama Rao, V.V.B. (1976). "The Creative Artist's Vision in Graham Greene's Novels." *Triveni*, 45, II, 55-62.

Richard, Kelly. (1984). *Graham Greene.* New York: Ungar.

Roy, North (1956). "Graham Greene." *Viswa Bharati Quarterly*, XXI, Spring, 376-99.

Spier, Ursula. (1957). "Melodrama in Graham Greene's *The End of the Affair.*" *Modern Fiction Studies*, Vol. III, No. 3, Autumn, 235-55.

Spitzer, L. (1948). *Linguistics and Literary History.* Princeton & New Jersey: Princeton University Press.

Stalnaker, Robert C. (1972). "Pragmatics." *Semantics of Natural Language*, ed. Donald Davidson & Gilbert Harman. New York: New York University Press, 197-214.

State, Audrey Nelson. (1960). "Technique and Form in the Novels of Graham Greene." *Dissertation Abstracts*, XXI, 629-30.

Sternberg, Meir. (1991). "How indirect discourse means." *Literary Pragmatics*, ed. Roger D. Sell. London & New York: Routledge.

Teun, A. Van Dijk. (1977). *Text and Context: Explorations in the Semantics and Pragmatics of Discourse.* London & New York: Longman.

Verchuren, J.E.F. and Marcella Berluccelli-Papi, ed. (1987). "The Pragmatic Perspective." Selected papers from the 1985 International Pragmatics Conference. (Pragmatics and beyond, Comparison Series 5) Amsterdam: Benjaminis.

Verdonik, Peter. (1988). "The Language of Poetry: The application of literary stylistic theory in University teaching" in Mike Short, ed., 241-66.

Vineberg, Steve. (1985). "The Harry Lime Mystery: Greene's *Third Man*. Screenplay." *Coll L*, 12 (1), 33-44.

Walker, Ronald C. (1973). "Seriation as Stylistic Norm in Graham Greene's *The End of the Affair*." *TSLL*, Summer, 26 (2), 218-41.

Watts, Richard J. (1981). *The Pragmalinguistic Analysis of Narrative Texts: Narrative Cooperation in Charles Dickens' "Hard Times."* Tubingem: Gunter Narr.

Wobbe, R.A. (1979). *Graham Greene: A Bibliography and Guide to Research* (GRCA 173). New York: Garland.